"We have known Loren and his lov
years. Having ministered in their church, LifeHouse, many times we have
found them to be two of the best encouragers around! We're certain that
you'll enjoy Loren's "God winks" with heartwarming, edifying, and at
times convicting stories! They're heartfelt, delightful, and easy to read
stories that everyone can identify with. This makes a great devotional!
Loren shares the Scriptures pertinent to the stories that parallel his own
life experiences and testimonies of God's faithfulness. Get ready to enjoy
this wonderful little book written by our amazing friend, Pastor Loren
Decker!"

Dr. Brian and Candice Simmons
The Passion Translation Project

"Over time, it's understandable how many of us become hardened,
cynical, and isolated. Our hearts are broken and we carry within us a
tremendous sense of being let down by the hopes we had and expectations
that life is wonderful, full of joy and love. Loren Decker is a beautiful
man who I've known most of my life. He lives his days and nights from
the inside out as a soul-connected, risk-taking believer in True Love. This
book of modern-day parables softens my heart and gives me further reason
to believe that God is real and actually loves me. Loren exemplifies what it
means to be a true pastor, a father, a husband, and a friend who has traveled
the extra mile with so many. This compilation of stories is evidence of a man
who counters this complex world with simple and honest truth, proving
God's love for us is actual, real, unconditional, and never ending. We are
never abandoned and we each can see and experience the strong hand of
love hidden in the shadows of life, especially when we love one another."

Dan Russell
New Sound Management, Soul Fest

I Love You, Church

Modern Parables

Loren Paul Decker
Senior Pastor of LifeHouse Church

I Love You, Church: Modern Parables
Copyright 2016 by Loren Paul Decker

Published by 5 Fold Media, LLC
www.5foldmedia.com

ISBN: 978-1-942056-28-7

Library of Congress Control Number: 2016943401

Printed in the United States of America

For Ash.

Acknowledgments

Thank you to my lovely wife, Amanda—you are my home and my family.

Thank you to my children who round out the rest of the Decker crew.

A special thanks to Brian and Candice Simmons.

I learned to appreciate the value of the teaching story (or parable) during my years working in Christian radio alongside Dr. John DeBrine of Songtime USA. The master of the "audio magazine" genre, John loved to use illustrations that would remain with the listener long after the broadcast was over. It was my job to find these vignettes and weave them into the radio program. John also taught me that the trials of life make you either better or bitter. Years later when I was diagnosed with Parkinson's Disease, those words rang in my memory as I determined to become better at my position as a pastor, my role as a dad, and as a husband to Amanda. For me, Parkinson's has not been a "beast," but it is a rather surly wild animal. Although I know that it passed through nail-scarred hands before it could reach me, for my life is in His hands. He gives grace in equal portion to any suffering He allows. Some of these modern parables find their roots in those old radio days. Thank you, Dr. John.

Thank you, Evangeline, for getting the project rolling and to Lydia for the many hours you spent helping me to make this book a reality.

Thank you, Dan and Ali, Jack, Maria, Aaron, Arturo, and Heather for reading the manuscript and making the suggestions and edits that transformed these stories into a book.

To Pastor Ed, CF, and Mr. "Kowalski" who supported me in this project, and to the many others who prayed and encouraged me.

Finally, thank you to all of my family at LifeHouse. I love you, Church!

Contents

Introduction

The term *parable* is one of those words that comes to us much as it was in the original Greek language. The two root words *para* and *bollo* combined mean "to throw alongside." By sharing a truth in story form, the reader finds it easier to understand a deeper point. This book contains a collection of modern parables from my life experiences. As you read them, they will come alongside your own life experience to underscore and illustrate truths that God will reveal.

I love you, church is a phrase I often voice to our congregation at LifeHouse. These stories were first told there in blogs, sermons, and conversations. But church is not limited to one place; rather, it is the coming together of all believers. Thus, in offering these parables my hope is that they will bless every one of you, whether you belong to a church or not. They are designed to cause you to reflect on God's love for each of us. I trust they will find a place in your own heart as together we journey into the very heart of God.

Peace and love,

Pastor Loren Paul Decker
Senior Pastor, LifeHouse Church

Losing Lane

"The Son of Man has come to seek out and to give life to those who are lost" (Luke 19:10).

It happened in an instant. I was standing in the checkout line with my two-year-old daughter, Lane, by my side. We were in Cape Cod and it was summertime—the store was packed. I was paying the bill, distracted for just a moment. Finished with my transaction, I reached down to take Lane by the hand—and she wasn't there.

"Did you see where my daughter went?" I asked the checkout person. She shrugged in indifference. Well, I was anything but indifferent. My daughter was missing!

I bumped my way back through the people standing in the checkout line, carving my way back into the store. My eyes scanned the crowd of shoppers, each one oblivious to my growing plight. I ducked low to look for little Lane, hoping to see her wandering in the crowd. I came up empty and my shock and anxiety grew even stronger. I began to dash up and down the aisles—but the more I looked, the more lost she became.

I started grabbing perfect strangers, asking for their help, hoping they had seen my little one. I rushed up to someone with a name tag and frantically asked her to lock the doors so that no one could escape with my Lane. Horrified by the thought, I ran outside myself to see if someone was getting into their car with my daughter. I was too panicked to be logical. I ran back into the store, feeling like I was going to throw up. I ran up the stairs to the second level, hurriedly asking everyone—anyone—to help search for my lost little girl.

Immediately after arriving on the second level, my heart sank. There before me were dozens of circular clothes racks, each one loaded with jackets and sweatshirts—so many places where a little child could hide! *I don't have time to look under each one*, I considered. *At least if she's up here under a clothes rack, she's not in the hands of some stranger*. I dashed back down the stairs. Minutes seemed like hours. My daughter was gone—we had searched the store, called her name—and still nothing. I found myself somewhere between shock and despair.

Just then, I saw her.

She was coming in the side entrance with her brother, returning from the penny candy store next door. Overwhelmed, I dropped to my knees and scooped up my little girl and held her close, tears falling down my cheeks. "I thought I had lost you. I thought someone had taken you away from me," I told her. I hung on to her with all that was in me. People clapped—happy endings call for that sort of thing.

Just then, while still on my knees, I heard my heavenly Father ask me, "Now, do you begin to understand how I feel about My children who are lost?"

If I had not already been on my knees, I would've sunk to them, the message was so strong and clear. Never again will I perceive a crowded store or street the same way. In those masses of strangers He is always there—calling, searching for His lost children. He came for that purpose—to seek and to save the lost. And He pleads for our help. How can we say no?

Geese

*"Yet the Lord longs to be gracious to you; therefore he will rise
up to show you compassion. For the Lord is a God of justice.
Blessed are all who wait for him!"* (Isaiah 30:18 NIV).

I heard the sound long before I could see them. My ears strained.
Beyond the crickets' whirring and above the occasional bark of a
neighborhood dog, the calls of a flock of geese could be faintly heard
in the night.

I was sitting on my porch, watching the full moon rise above the tree
line. That seems to be my spot in the evenings—a peaceful place to reflect
and pray. My yard seems bigger at night, the woods providing a dark
frame for the creatures of the night who share my address with me. The
moon was up now, reflecting light and casting shadows.

They were closer now, clearly heading in my direction. I could picture
them before I could see them. A flock of Canada geese, in a perfect V,
were practicing for their long journey to their southern home. They go
there each winter when the cold air comes north to New England. My
eyes strained in the night—so close now.

Often on my drive to work, I pass another flock of Canada geese that
seem to enjoy the environs of a particular cranberry bog in my hometown.
There they gather by the dozens, honking and pecking, flapping and
scratching—I guess geese like cranberries. Sometimes I fling a piece of
bread or a stale donut their way. I get a kick out of watching the mayhem
that erupts at the sight of a jelly stick coming at them. The flock moves as
one for the goal then settles down quickly after the food supply is gone.

One such day it was different. As I drove past the bog, I saw but one goose—a lone figure standing. He looked to be lost and confused and gingerly walked around, craning his neck as if to say, "Where'd everybody go?" Perhaps he overslept and missed roll call that day, or maybe he returned from a trip only to find the flock had moved on, or maybe he got nipped by a fellow goose in a scrap over a jelly donut and his feelings were hurt. I don't speak "goose" so I couldn't ask him. Nonetheless, he surely seemed vulnerable as I drove slowly past.

So here is my bog/geese/goose application. The enemy wants to isolate you—cutting you off from the family. He will lie, mislead, and derail you to cause you to feel alone. There is, however, strength in numbers—and we were meant to travel together. By ourselves we lose our purpose and our way. "Where did everybody go?" can be a question born of self-pity, or it can be a measurement of our motivation to catch up with the "flock," to take our place in the family.

Back to my porch vigil in the night. Suddenly, there they were! Dark outlines against the moon, calling to each other—geese on the wing in the night sky. I held my breath. No one else on the planet would see this scene of natural beauty. I thanked God for allowing me this moment to be alive.

Christian, can you hear the sounds of blessing drawing closer and closer? The book of Isaiah says, "The Lord longs to be gracious to you" (Isa. 30:18 NIV). Our spiritual ears strain, and yes! Grace is surely headed our way. You can see it before it comes into view—the blessing of God on His people, it is coming. Unlike my private view of the geese silhouetted against the moon, it is there for all of us to see. It is reason to say, "Thank you, God, for allowing me this moment to be alive."

Hold your breath. So close now!

Snapshots

"Throughout the coming ages will be the visible display of the infinite, limitless riches of his grace and kindness, which was showered upon us in Jesus Christ" (Ephesians 2:7a).

We've been taking a lot of pictures at the Decker home lately. There have been trips taken to Florida, Soul Fest, and Horseneck Beach—and of course, we never tire of snapping candid shots of the youngest ones and their antics. Suffice it to say, I have been flipping through a lot of photos.

Now, I can't prove this scientifically, and my only evidence is anecdotal, but I have noticed something interesting about us as humans. Think with me—when observing a picture of a group of people, who do we look for first? Right—ourselves. More often than not, we sneak a quick glance our own way to see "how it came out." How does our hair look (a moot point for me)? How goofy is our smile? How tubby are we getting to be these days (not a moot point for me)?

Back to the photos. After quick but careful analysis of "us," we expand our view to see the whole gang and decide if anyone else is going to see this print. The *only* time that I know of when we look at ourselves *after* viewing someone else is when the photo involves our children. If there's a picture snapped of me holding sleeping baby True on the couch, I always "ooh and aah" over how cute he is *before* I ever look my own way. I look to see my daughter Evangeline opening her birthday gift with delight before noticing my pleasured expression in the background—guaranteed.

We always love to see pictures of ourselves reflected in our children. It inspires us to measure their lives in single beautiful moments, stilled by the camera's eye. That's as it should be. "She looks just like her dad," thrills me far more than any photo of me ever could.

Still thinking with me? How much joy, then, does it provide our heavenly Father when one of our captured life moments reflects His very image in us? His family album is full of snapshots of you and me. His eyes scan the backdrop of His earth, looking for great moments in the lives of His children. And there they are, stuck up on His fridge—a bunch of goofy smiles. We are loved children of God, first in the Father's heart. Yes, He loves us first. Think about that. Never doubt the importance of worship. It gets our eyes off of ourselves and puts them squarely on God. The trick is to live that way!

I heard a great story the other day in my pastor's fellowship group. It seems there was a group of esteemed philosophers and theologians at a Bible conference years ago. An impromptu discussion broke out in one of the hallways outside one of the lectures. The subject was, "What sets Christianity apart from other world religions?"

As the group of high-minded thinkers pontificated and set forth their lengthy answers, someone noticed that the author C.S. Lewis was passing by. Looking to draw him into the discussion, one theologian posed the question, "Lewis, what makes Christianity different from the other world religions?" Without missing a step or a beat, the author replied, "Grace," and kept walking.

We are recipients of great, passionate grace, but with the grace comes the responsibility to live up to such a noble calling. We are representatives—snapshots, if you will—of God's deep investment in humankind. Our character carries the message—we are recipients of love. Now, say cheese!

True Love

*"For the greatest love of all is a love that sacrifices all. And this
great love is demonstrated when a person sacrifices his life for
his friends"* (John 15:13).

"True love always manifests itself in sacrifice toward the object of its affections" was a quote I learned from an old friend of mine, radio host John DeBrine. I have seen it ring true over the course of my years—rarely as clearly as on a school bus route in my home town.

My daughter Mercedes rode the bus each morning on her way to middle school. Her assigned seat was near the back of the bus, where the "cool" kids sat—or so she thought. As the first few weeks of school went by, it became apparent that a girl near the front of the bus had become the focus of derision. The "pack in back" teased her mercilessly, often reducing her to tears.

At first, Mercedes joined in the bully behavior, but day by day it wore on her conscience. Finally she summoned her courage. "Let's lay off the teasing," she managed. "It's not right!" Well, the teasing and cruel talk continued—but now there were two targets, the girl down front and Mercedes in the rear.

One night at the dinner table, Mercedes inquired if I could ask the bus driver for a new seating assignment for her. Understanding the situation at hand, I assured her that I would speak to the driver in the morning. The next day that's just what I did. The bus driver was agreeable. "Pick any seat you'd like," he told my daughter. So she boarded the big yellow school bus with the jeers ringing in her ears. What happened next surprised us all. Mercedes chose her new seat—right beside the lonely young girl who had been teased so badly all year long. There they sat, enduring the taunts together.

Later that day in the school hallway, Mercedes was passing by a group headed in the opposite direction. One young girl broke from the group, ran over to Mercedes and hugged her tightly. It was her new friend from the bus.

You and I have been loved like that. Jesus came to earth to be one with us. He sat with us, ate with us, and spoke with us. Taunts and sneers came His way, but He shook them off and came closer still. He shared our seat. He loved us—truly. You are not alone, not anymore.

Mrs. B.

"For the blessing granted us through the prayers of many"
(2 Corinthians 1:11b ESV).

H er name was Mrs. Bynum, and she managed the bookstore when I was at Gordon College. I didn't spend much time in the bookstore (I should've spent more time in the actual books for that matter!) while I was a student there, so how is it that to this day I often recall Mrs. Bynum? Let me explain.

One morning while in my senior year at Gordon I was purchasing a newspaper in the bookstore, and from behind the counter Mrs. Bynum asked, "Loren, do you have time for me to buy you a cup of coffee?" Well, we'd never shared much more than a "hello" prior to that morning, but I heard myself answer, "Sure." Honestly, I figured that I must've done something wrong and was about to hear about it. What I did hear that morning changed my life.

We walked together to the coffee shop and found a quiet corner. "Mrs. B" sat across a table from me and proceeded to tell me how each new school year the Lord would place one student from the freshman class on her heart to pray for every day. Four years earlier, I had been that student. I listened in stunned silence as she shared with me how she had prayed for me every morning for the past four years. She told me things God had put on her heart about me and how she faithfully brought them before the throne. I am absolutely certain that one of the reasons that I am pastor today is an answer to Mrs. Bynum's daily prayers.

One advantage of living for fifty-plus years is realizing how valuable time truly is. Most things we learn (and grow from) transpire over many days. Moments of revelation are treasured, but change usually comes over time. Each of us is on a lifetime journey, and the walk of the disciple is just that—a walking journey into truth. The problem is that we all like things to occur in instantaneous fashion, and we tend to get frustrated when things require more than an instant.

A number of years ago, a major sports team partnered with a charitable organization in order to donate thousands of articles of clothing to Third World nations. They all read "2011 Champs!" Of course, you guessed it, that team didn't win the big game, but the merchandisers needed to print up winning memorabilia for both squads, knowing that consumers would want to purchase the items immediately after the game was over. Unless they had them available, sales would be lost. People want their results in fast fashion. Mrs. B knew better. She was patient to pray for four years before saying a word to me.

One of the fruits of the Spirit is patience. It's also first on the apostle Paul's list of defining what love is. Love is patient. God is not in a rush. That person you are praying for is in a lifetime process with God, and while it's important to measure progress, real changes may take some time. This is not a personal excuse for us to lie in the doldrums and remain stationary in our spiritual journey, but it is a reminder that instant results often end up like those donated championship jerseys—not really accurate. A patient approach to life (ours or someone else's) will never go to waste.

Let's hold each other up in prayer like Mrs. B. did for me. When the apostle Paul wrote to the Corinthian church, he thanked them for praying and said, "You are helping us by praying for us" (2 Corinthians 1:11 NLT). Ask God to bring someone to your mind and heart today and patiently pray, pray, pray!

Any Loose Change?

"Therefore, we are ambassadors for Christ, God making his appeal through us. We implore you on behalf of Christ, be reconciled to God" (2 Corinthians 5:20 ESV).

Before I was a pastor I worked in Christian radio as producer and co-host of a nationally syndicated program. I enjoyed the work, especially our affiliation with the Billy Graham Evangelistic Association. We would often travel to broadcast live from crusade sites, and then following the meetings we would remain on the air in the region, teaching basic Bible truths to the many converts who were growing in their newfound faith. The Graham team was always friendly and supportive. Interviews with the "regulars" were easy to arrange and always inspirational. Crusade guests were also readily accessible and always gracious with their time.

My most unforgettable encounter with Dr. Graham's organization, however, came not in an interview with someone famous, but rather with a behind-the-scenes gentleman whose name you would not know. He traveled with the team as a media representative and we quickly became friends. I'll call him "Mr. S."

The crusade site was in the Arco Arena in Sacramento, California. I was traveling with a friend of our ministry. Together with Mr. S, our behind-the-scenes media friend, we made a decision to rent an automobile and take a day to drive down the coast and visit San Francisco. I had never been to that city, and I was looking forward to seeing the Golden Gate Bridge and Alcatraz. The three of us hit the city mid-morning and began to take in the sights. Down by the waterfront we watched the harbor seals and enjoyed the fresh air.

"I'm hungry," said Mr. S. "Let's get a bite to eat."

"Here's a diner," I suggested.

As we approached the entrance, we saw him. A homeless man, tin cup extended, begging. "Any loose change?" he called out from his place near the front door.

We stood before him—our business suits a stark contrast to his rags. I spoke up, "Let us buy you lunch," I offered the homeless gentleman.

"Come on in and sit with us!" added my friend.

He responded that although he was grateful for the offer, he had to turn it down. He explained that his place there by the entrance of that eatery was "prime turf" for panhandlers and that he had been lucky to get that spot today. He said that if he left his post another would be sure to grab it.

"How about I hold your place for you?" I looked at Mr. S as he spoke. "You go ahead and eat while I stay out here and hold your spot." Days beyond his last good meal, the homeless man accepted. And there stood Mr. S from the Billy Graham team, tin cup in hand, calling "Any loose change?" When we came out of the restaurant about an hour later, Mr. S was still at it. He had been ridiculed and spat on. He had been cursed to his face by those objecting to a man in a fine suit panhandling for spare change. Unfazed and undaunted, he stood his ground. "I kept your spot," said he to the homeless man. "Any loose change?" he called again to the crowd.

I stood in wonder as the two men switched back their places. For the rest of that day—indeed for the rest of my life—I have known what compassion truly looks like. It isn't kindness from a distance—it is standing in the gap, being the voice for one less fortunate and pleading with the passersby, "Any loose change?" I can also picture the cross at Calvary with clearer focus.

For Someone came and visited my city one day long ago. He stood in my place so that I might have a seat at the table.

Revelation

"God said to Moses, 'I am who I am'" (Exodus 3:14 NIV).

There's a lot we don't know—especially when it comes to God. Oh, we like to think we have Him figured out, wrapped nicely in a theological box or denominational package. But if we are truly honest, I think we would have to admit that some of what we arrive at in our "knowing" is actually what we *hope* God is like. We end up serving a God with whom we are comfortable—or more likely, having Him serve us.

This much I do know: what we can understand about God is called revelation (what He shows us). Our Father is the ultimate "revealer" of truth, letting our hearts grasp what we need to comprehend and leaving the rest to mystery, worship, and awe-filled wonder.

Some of the most interesting revelations about who God is come from knowing His names in Scripture. Names mean a lot in the Bible. At one point, God shares His name with Moses and tells him that it means, "I AM." Now, if I told you that my name was "I am" you'd logically ask the following question. "I am, what?" Well, the Lord fills in that blank beautifully. Let me show you how.

There are three basic names that God chose to reveal His character in the Scriptures. (There are other variations and compound usages, but that is a more complete or exhaustive study. Knowing God is a lifelong quest!) The following is a simple study guide to help when reading God's Word. You may want to take some notes to keep in your Bible!

Name 1: Elohim—Translated in your Bible as "God" (Genesis 1:1). Definition: "The Strong One."

Name 2: Adonnai—Translated in your Bible as "Lord" (Exodus 4:10). Definition: "Owner/Master."

Name 3: YHWH—Translated in your Bible as "Lord" (Exodus 3:14-15). Definition: "I am."

These three names are found throughout Scripture. YHWH is given or written as Jehovah and is the exclusive name that God shares with no one (see Ps. 83:18).

There are certain combination forms of the exclusive name for the Lord that help fill in the blank about who He is: "I am _____" (spellings may vary).

- Jehovah-Jireh (Genesis 22:14): "Provider"
- Jehovah-Raphaka (or Rapha) (Exodus 15:26): "Healer"
- Jehovah-Shalom (Judges 6:24): "Peace"
- Jehovah-Zidkenu (or Tsedkeh) (Jeremiah 23:6): "Righteousness"
- Jehovah-Shammah (Ezekiel 48:35): "Present with us"
- Jehovah-Roah (Psalms 23:1): "Shepherd"
- Jehovah-Nissi (Exodus 17:15): "Captain, Conqueror, Banner"
- Jehovah-Sabaoth (James 5:4): "Commander of Hosts (heavenly armies)"

YHWH finally filled in *all* the blanks with one final name—*Jesus* (see John 18:5-6). The person of Christ fulfills the characteristics of Jehovah as revealed in His names. He is God's provision as the Lamb of God and the Bread of Life. His healings demonstrated His authority over disease. He said, "My peace I leave with you." He is described in 1 John as Jesus Christ, the righteous. He said He would always be with us. He is the Good Shepherd. He always leads us in triumph and He could have called legions of angels to deliver Him from the cross. But He didn't—because the ultimate revelation is His Love.

When you are praying, don't just start with "Dear God." That's not really His name! If you're in need of peace, call Him Jehovah-Shalom. If you're in need of healing, direct your prayer by saying Jehovah-Raphaka. And if you're short on supplies, call on Jehovah-Jireh. The Lord reveals His names for a purpose—so that we can know Him better. Are you on a first-name basis with Him?

Division Street

"I want the little children to come to me, so never interfere with them when they want to come, for heaven's kingdom realm is composed of beloved ones like these" (Matthew 19:14).

It seemed like a good summer job. A friend and I would go "half-sies" on an ice cream truck—each of us doing three full days a week and alternating Sundays after church. The idea worked pretty well. My partner was a hustler—I was more social. Together, we developed a successful route in the city.

Despite having three beaches on our route, I enjoyed driving through the projects the best. I was known to the neighborhood kids as "Flash," a nickname I had acquired the previous summer as a camp counselor.

"Flash! I got thirty-five cents. What can I buy?" The question would often be accompanied by a fistful of change—dumped in my open window.

I would make a pretense of counting it before saying, "Anything on my truck—you've got it." (I drove my partner crazy.)

Division Street was my favorite street. There was a large group of youngsters who lived there and their laughter was contagious. I would park the truck, climb out the service window, and get involved in an impromptu game of kickball or soccer until the clock said it was way past time to leave.

It was on one such day when I first saw the two boys. Standing behind an iron gate about fifteen feet from the curb where my truck was parked, two timid young lads stood stoically watching the activity around my visit. They were neatly dressed, crisp white shirts, shorts, and suspenders, socks pulled up high. I was certain they would like a cool treat so I asked, "Ice cream, boys?" With a frightened glance toward each other, they turned and ran as fast as their little legs would carry them. Up the back stairs I heard them go, calling for "Mama" and excitedly talking loudly in a foreign language to whoever intercepted them inside their apartment.

The next day they were back—watching from a safe distance, yet again retreating quickly from my ice cream offers. As the summer wore on, I got nowhere with the pair. But as August began to blend into September I grew even more determined to gain their trust.

On one of my last days on the route I waited until the crowd had cleared on Division Street. I dug into the freezer and pulled out two of my best ice cream treats. I trotted up to the fence extending the ice cream treats in my hands. "For you!" I said. Too shocked (or too curious) to run, they accepted my offering—and then bolted up the back stairs. The breeze carried the sound of excited conversation from the upstairs window. I could not understand the language—not one word—so I put the truck in gear, released the brake, and drove to my next stop.

The next day was my last. I did the beach routes and the park—but my mind was on Division Street. When I finally arrived there it was evening. The sun was low in the sky and a breeze carrying hints of autumn blew through the brick buildings. I pulled up to my usual stop and got out to say goodbye to the crowd of kids. No sign of my small friends. I high-fived my last customer and turned the key in the ignition.

I took one last look toward the iron gate only to see it swing open as a beautiful young woman came hurriedly toward my truck, her two little boys in tow. I realized this was "Mama" and she was on a mission. I swung out of the driver's seat and met her at the window. With a glance back at her boys she handed me a piece of paper that I recognized to be public assistance food stamps.

"I can't accept these," I said, shaking my head no. She was nodding yes with a glare.

"You take. For ice cream!" she said with such determination, I knew arguing was pointless. She was going to pay for those two ice creams from the day before and her boys and I knew it.

I accepted the currency and put it in my jeans pocket—it would have been pointless to put it in with the day's sales.

When I think back to that summer, I don't remember how much money I made or how many miles I logged on that old truck. I do, however think about those ice cream treats placed in the hands of two brothers who were, most likely, spending their first summer in America.

I'm certain there are families surrounding all of us who are feeling alienated and frightened. We can change their experience with a small gift given in love. Jesus said even a cup of cold water given in His name would never be overlooked in the kingdom. He also said it is better to give than receive. I'll vouch for that.

I still hold onto the memory of that immigrant family to this day. I often wonder what those two boys grew up to be. I'm sure that when they finally ventured beyond that little iron gate on Division Street they were well prepared to earn their way—that's if Mama had anything to do with it.

As for Mama, she would be an old woman now—one, I hope, with the fond memory of an ice cream truck driver's kindness to her two boys. I hope she smiles at the recollection of that day. And, too, I hope that somehow it made a very foreign place feel a little more like home for her and her family. After all, we are all foreigners in one way or another. We are just passing through this life; the days fade like the memories of summers long ago. As the years roll on, we collect memories and keepsakes to remind us that life can be wonderful. We share the awe as we watch it pass, like two lads who were watching their first-ever encounter with an ice cream truck. The wonder should never leave us, like little children. The King awaits, arms extended, and what He is holding out for us is far better than ice cream. But He won't accept payment either—the price has already been paid.

Ginger Ale

"Since all his 'children' have flesh and blood, so Jesus became fully human to fully identify with us. He did this, so that he could experience death and annihilate the effects of the intimidating accuser who holds against us the power of death" (James 2:14).

My wife, Amanda, came down with the stomach bug early one morning, so I spent the day at home, taking care of the needs there. I ran to the store and bought my wife a big bottle of ginger ale, made toast, did the dishes—and of course, changed the diapers of my almost-two-year-old, True. Small stuff, I know, but it was a great day because I felt honored to be able to do some simple, tangible acts that say "I love you" to my family. I should do that every day, not just when Amanda is ill. It got me thinking.

Sometimes we get caught between our knowing and our doing. Remember what David did when he faced the giant, Goliath, in front of him? He stood his ground. Because David didn't flee, "the whole world knew that there was a God in Israel." Our faith actions are our testimony! The church is made up of individuals who are finding that His strength shows up in our lives, our families, our relationships, and our day-to-day experiences—one choice at a time. That's what we teach at LifeHouse. Our Christianity is lived out ten minutes at a time. Do the next right thing before you. Small steps will lead to a pathway, and along that way you will discover the journey that will take you into the very heart of God. The Bible isn't a theory—it's a how-to manual. We are to be good listeners of the Word, and we should be getting better all the time at being good "doers."

Scripture shows us that our faith has to be matched by works in order to count. Also, Colossians 1:9-10 illustrates that our faith must be grounded firmly in the true knowledge of God in order to produce positive action ("You'll grow as you get to know God better and better"). In other words, we will be more consistent in our walk when we have our minds and our hearts set on God. We are "doers" by nature. When I taught Evangeline (or any of my children) how to tie her shoes, I showed her once and then it became "Let me do it!" as her little fingers grabbed at the laces. When we learn, we want to do—so as we learn the way of truth, we must apply it. This is not head knowledge faith. Rather, it is heart-felt decisions being played out on the stage of our lives for an audience of One.

"Suppose a brother or a sister is without clothes and daily food. If one of you says to them, 'Go in peace; keep warm and well fed,' but does nothing about their physical needs, what good is it?" (James 2:15-16 NIV). So if God-like, God-pleasing behavior from us is to *fulfill* a need for one who asks, it surely illustrates that God will fulfill our request to know more of Him in tangible, actual ways that will make an immediate impact on our lives. Ask Him for the strength and courage to do that next right thing before you. If you ask Him for bread, He won't offer you a stone.

So with the Word as our authority, there will be times in my life today when God will call me to show love for Him. He doesn't personally need a cup of cold water (or a bottle of ginger ale), but the beauty is that when I see that someone else does, He counts it as a service to Him. Let's join together and find the place where God is asking us to let our lives display that there is a God in charge and that He is mighty and strong! We should feel honored to have a family chore or two before us. They could be mountains that loom huge, or just little things that require a patient attitude. Either way, let's live above our feelings and not beneath our circumstances! In doing so, we surely will knock off a giant or two! Ten minutes at a time.

Busboy Mentality

*"For even the Son of Man did not come expecting to be
served by everyone, but to serve everyone, and to give his
life as the ransom price in exchange for the salvation of
many"* (Mark 10:45).

When I was a teenager, I belonged to the youth group at church. A good group it was, lots of fun and games and plenty of Bible study. Occasionally we would go on a retreat where we would compete with other youth from the region in a weekend-long struggle for youth group supremacy. These were grand times. We squared off against our young rivals in any number of sports competitions and games, the weekend winner receiving a trophy of significant proportions for proud display back at their home church. For the rest of us, it was always "Wait 'til next year."

As we waited, we also prepared for the following year. Part of that preparation was to raise enough money to pay for the next year's trip. Part of preparing for that trip was the annual "slave day" where we raked or mowed, cleaned, or painted for those church members who were willing to donate to our cause after a full day of chores. No one ever really liked slave day—it isn't much fun to be a servant. In hindsight, however, it was probably the best preparation for life that we ever encountered—youth retreats included.

Jesus called twelve men—men who soon developed grand schemes of powerful future positions in Messiah's government. Yet, instead of civics lessons and sword drills, Jesus had them serving lunch to the masses and—even worse—cleaning up afterward. You know the story well; Jesus and His posse were in vacation mode, planning to get away and relax for a few days. However, thousands still gathered on the hills outside of Jerusalem to hear the Rabbi. Jesus obliged and began to teach while the disciples fumed. So captivated were the masses by the simple yet profound doctrine that they remained for hours. As the day wore on, hunger set in and restlessness crept through the crowd. Noting the distraction, Jesus ordered His disciples to scurry up some lunch.

"Impossible," said the twelve. "What are we supposed to feed them?" they asked Jesus. The questions muttered under their breath most likely carried an even more sarcastic tone. "Send them away to fend for themselves." The disciples' distaste for their assignment was more than obvious.

"I want you to feed them," Jesus insisted. And He sent them into the crowd to see if they could find enough food supplies to feed everyone. One little lad had a lunch of five bread loaves and a couple of fish—not enough for the small army of hungry folks along the hillside. The rest of the story is miraculous. Jesus thanked His Father for the lunch and began to divide it evenly amongst the amazed disciples. Not only was there enough for all, there were twelve baskets of leftovers!

Now, if you or I were there for that miracle, I would think we would be standing, mouths agape saying, "Do that again—you know, the part with the bread? And the thing with the fish—amazing! How did You do it, Jesus?" Not the disgruntled disciples. They were humiliated that they had to serve commoners lunch when in their minds they should be ruling over them. As a result, the Twelve missed the miracle—blinded by ambition and self-pity. That seems to be how the Bible reports this episode.

A short time later the scene repeats—thousands of hungry men and women, with Jesus teaching straight through lunch and people getting restless.

"He's going to make us do the serving thing *again*," the twelve surmised. But this time when Jesus asked what was on hand for food, He didn't have to send them into the crowd to check what food was available. They had already taken stock and knew how much was on hand (a few fish and some bread again). Everything was in readiness for a second miracle—a "do over" if you will, and still the disciples' refrain was, "Send them away." Instead, Jesus sent them back into the crowd, miracle food in hand and reluctance in their collective hearts. The cleanup duty fell on their shoulders as well. It would be akin to cleaning out the school bus after the weekend youth retreat—cheeseburger wrappers, Styrofoam cups, soda cans, and smashed French fries. Enough to fill seven trash bags!

Later in their boat while crossing the Galilean Sea, Jesus warned the disciples not to have a heart like a Pharisee. A Pharisee, according to Jesus, could tell you what to do but would never lift a finger to help. Pride can cause that kind of heart to sneak in pretty easily. The Lord knew that well. But when you're at the bottom—a servant—there isn't much chance for pride to steal the show—or your heart for that matter. So I say, let's leave the teaching to Jesus while the rest of us become bread passers and busboys—service with a smile. No need to struggle for supremacy. That score is settled. Jesus wins.

As for us, well, we don't get a trophy to put in the church lobby for being a slave, but there promises to be a crown someday!

A Close Call

"'For I know the plans I have for you,' says the Lord. 'They are plans for good and not for disaster, to give you a future and a hope'" (Jeremiah 29:11 NLT).

My wife lost her car keys the other day. We hunted, searched, dug under sofa cushions, crawled into cubby holes where baby True might have taken them—we turned the house upside down. My friend even broke into the car in case we had left the keys inside when we locked it up for the night. We searched trash cans and cupboards—no keys anywhere. "I'm going to be so late," Amanda said in frustration.

I drove Amanda to work in my car and picked her up again at the close of her workday. "I searched everywhere," I told her. "No sign of them." When we got home, Amanda placed her gear down on the kitchen counter, moving a folder in the process.

There they were—as plain as day under a paper folder that we must have moved a dozen times in our search. My mind immediately went to the Lord's protection over us. Those keys, I believe, were kept from our eyes in order to keep my wife's car in the driveway for the day. Who but God knows what peril on the highway was avoided because of our "key delay"?

It happened again a few days ago. Prudence was unusually slow getting ready for school. We urged her to hustle—but she just seemed stuck in low gear. Upon finally getting out the door, my wife drove her along the familiar route to school. Just after getting on the highway, they came upon a six-car pileup that had just occurred. Rescue vehicles were just arriving on the scene. The pair couldn't help but wonder—what would have happened if they had left on time?

Years ago when I was a teenager, my buddy DW purchased a four-wheel-drive vehicle. We couldn't wait to off-road it, and so that first night in the new machine we headed out for Snow's Pond and the dirt roads that surrounded it. The roads were single file in that area—little more than paths. If you ever met a vehicle coming in your direction, both cars would have to maneuver two wheels up on the embankment and inch by each other in that fashion. Slow was the only safe speed on these back roads. That night, however, DW opened the throttle and we barreled down the drive—much faster than we should have. We bumped and swayed, jostling in our seats—barely under control. Suddenly we hit a hollow in the road and lost what little control we had—sideswiping a tree and snapping off the passenger side mirror before careening to a halt. We got out to inspect the damage. The broken mirror had smashed the passenger window, and a deep crease in the truck body ran the length of the vehicle. Incredibly, the metal gas cap was found (we had our flashlights out) imbedded in a tree trunk. DW was upset. We were both a little shaken.

We climbed back in our banged-up truck and decided to turn around and head for home—enough adventure for one night. Or so we thought. As we limped along slowly, looking for a place to turn, we rounded a bend in the path and came upon a car parked in the middle of the dirt road, lights off and packed full of teenagers. We jerked to a stop, inches from their front bumper. They had found a place to party in secret—in the dark, far off the beaten path. It nearly was disastrous. Had we not lost control and sideswiped a tree a few hundred yards up the road, we would have crashed into that darkened car, loaded with teens, at about fifty miles per hour. I am certain lives would have been lost.

So the next time you lose your keys, experience a delay, or have a small mishap, stop and thank God for keeping you from a far greater loss. What He has kept us from, we may never know. Our heavenly Father sees the road ahead. He knows the steps we will take, and He goes before us—occasionally hiding the keys. Our disappointments are His appointments.

Bare Feet

"God sends angels with special orders to protect you wherever you go, defending you from all harm. If you walk into a trap, they'll be there for you and keep you from stumbling!" (Psalms 91:11-12).

I heard the crash. *That's a bad one*, I thought. I hadn't heard the squeal of brakes before the impact, so all I could think of was "head-on."

We lived on a major route where traffic flowed freely, and accidents—although rare—were sometimes tragic.

It was a summer day, and it had been raining hard all morning. As I headed for the door, I was intercepted by Karen, a friend of ours from the community. "There's been a terrible accident, and I think it's Carl and my kids," she said breathlessly.

Carl was an old and dear friend, and my mind raced as his wife explained. They had left the house within minutes of each other and Carl was just ahead of her car with the children riding in the van with him. Was that loud crash from his vehicle? With Karen right behind me I flew out the door, never stopping to put on shoes. I ran barefoot through the puddles—the highway seemed more like a river than a street. Traffic had already come to a standstill and I could see an ambulance pulling up to the crash scene. "That's our van!" cried Karen as we got close. There was devastation and wreckage everywhere. I saw an EMT loading a child into the ambulance, "You go with the ambulance, I'll stay with Carl," I managed to say. Karen quickly ran to the emergency vehicle while I tried to take in the scene before me.

Rescue workers were arriving and police cars were everywhere it seemed.

"Help!"

I heard the cry coming from the twisted metal. I recognized the voice as Carl's. My thoughts a blur, I shouted "Clergy!" to an officer as I climbed over the back of the car. I crawled onto the roof and slid down toward the crumpled end. The windshield was gone, so I lay across the hood (or what was left of it) and reached in. "Take my hand!" I hollered to Carl.

"Loren, is that you?" he moaned.

"Yes!" I screamed, "I've got you buddy." I held on and started to pray. The rain was soaking all of us and chaos was all around. Carl and I held on for dear life.

The jaws of life were brought out to try and cut off the metal prison my friend was in. Every inch seemed to produce more pain in Carl's broken body. A blanket was thrown over his legs, but I could see the damage was severe.

"Are the kids okay?" Carl yelled.

"Yes, they're with Karen!" I said in his ear.

The moments seemed like hours. We held on tightly and I prayed out loud.

"Loren, are the kids okay?" Carl cried out again. Shock was obviously taking over.

"Yes, they're safe," I repeated.

Finally the metal was removed and they carefully began to take Carl's injured body from the wreckage. He screamed in pain—my tears ran with the rain.

"We got him, Loren," said a friend of mine on the force.

"Are the kids okay?" Carl begged again as they placed him in the back of the ambulance.

"Safe and sound," I whispered—more to myself than to anyone around me.

I climbed down from the wreck, amid broken glass and twisted metal. The road was flooded with the rain. While the ambulance pulled away, I walked back to my home where Amanda stood waiting on the porch. As we huddled together, I looked down at my bare feet and noted with amazement, "Not even one scratch!" I had just walked barefoot through the worst accident scene I had ever known. The God of heaven cared about my feet that day as I walked through disaster.

Oh, the love of Jesus—the unselfish love that caused Him to cry, even in the face of certain death on the cross. "Are the kids okay?"

"Yes, yes, Jesus, we are—we're okay." Even our bare feet tell the story of love.

—

Memories of Mom

"Your crucifixion with Christ has severed the tie to this life, and now your true life is hidden away in God as you live within the Anointed One" (Colossians 3:3).

I t was the day before we would hold a memorial service for my mom. She left the nursing home for heaven on a cold morning in March. Leafing through her collection of photographs, I couldn't help but consider the words of Jesus, "I am the way, the truth, and the life." My mom found the way as a young lady, and her life bore testimony to the fact that what she had discovered was indeed true. The pictures tell the story: friends, family, church, camp, home—my mother drank deeply from the fountain of life, and it splashed over into every part of her existence. She never relied on the world for much of anything. It did not sustain her. Jesus did.

That's the way it should be, I reckon. Isaiah 53 (the incredible prophecy of the suffering Messiah) reads that Jesus, the Servant, grew up like a tender shoot in dry ground. If a green plant is in dry ground, it cannot draw sustenance from its environment. The parched earth offers no hope for life-giving nourishment. Worldly sources do little to satisfy. But Jesus said, "My kingdom is not of this world." He drew life support from another place, and He offers that same support to those who believe.

A few weeks before my mom's memorial service, I walked out of church on Sunday and noticed a group of our people standing in the center of the parking lot, eyes shielded against the bright blue sky—staring upward. They were pointing excitedly to something high over the church.

It was an eagle. Sure enough, there soaring high above us was the very symbol of strength and protection itself—a beautiful eagle.

My mind went to the verse recorded by the ancient prophet, Isaiah 40:31 (NRSV), "But those who wait for the Lord shall renew their strength, they shall mount up with wings like eagles, they shall run and not be weary, they shall walk and not faint." The admonition in Isaiah is to "wait upon" the Lord. The words mean "to bind together," to be so thoroughly enmeshed in Him that we hardly know where we end and He begins. It means we have abandoned our purposes for His guidance. It means we have exchanged our heart for His.

So, when we honored the life of Ruth Decker, we really weren't celebrating her at all. Instead, we were bringing honor to the Lord Jesus— the unseen reality in all of the fading photographs. If you look, you really can't miss Him. As the Scriptures say, "My life is hidden in Christ."

Mom, you hid yourself well, and I've got pictures and memories to prove it.

New Glasses

"Be free from pride-filled opinions, for they will only harm your cherished unity. Don't allow self-promotion to hide in your hearts, but in authentic humility put others first and view others more important than yourself. Abandon every shallow display of selfishness. Possess a greater concern for what matters to others instead of your own interests" (Philippians 2:3-4).

I am now bespectacled. I have acquired eyewear. My eyes have need of corrective lenses. In short, I got glasses—bifocals to boot. My wife tells me they are "nerd chic," although there is really nothing chic about them. I just know that now I can actually see. What was fuzzy is now clear. There is definition to my sight—I have gained visual perspective.

What is alarming is what I had gotten used to. I didn't know how poor my sight had become because it was, well, my sight. Until the doctor put the prescriptive remedy to my face, I was somewhat blind—but didn't know it. Now that trees have individual leaves, I realize what I had been missing. Now I will know the price at the gas pump before I pull in to refuel. Think of the many pluses I have gained!

The application is all too obvious. We all tend to get comfortable with our own perspectives. Yet when the Lord shows us things through the corrective lens of His Word, our world is suddenly defined by a new clarity and focus. It's a little cumbersome at first. You must remember to put your glasses on in order to benefit from their correction. You must take them with you (and remember where you left them!). It's the same with divine perspective. You must choose to put it on. You may even appear a little "nerdy," but once you become used to it—you never want to go "fuzzy" again.

Perspective.

I awoke the other night and had some quiet time with the Lord; it was one of those "wee hours of the morning" encounters—you know the ones. I was asking Him about spiritual maturity and what it means to be pleasing to Him, no matter what it takes. So Jesus taught me this little lesson:

Picture yourself on a dream vacation in a deluxe hotel. You've come to get away, but on the first night you discover that you have noisy neighbors next door. Their crashes, bangs, door slams, and loud voices keep you from your rest. What would you do? Call the manager and complain? Pound on the wall? Go and knock on their door and insist that they quiet down? Patience would surely run thin.

Now switch the scene to a hospital room. A slim curtain separates you from your neighbor. All night long from that next bed comes moaning, groaning, and violent coughing. A never-ending stream of medical professionals are in and out of the room with crash carts and responding to alarms—but you would never dream of demanding that they keep quiet. Why not? The simple truth is, that is the nature of a hospital and the patient *needs* to be there. You most likely would find yourself praying for that noisy neighbor as the night wears on.

Jesus pointed me to the church and said, "We are to be a hospital for the sick, not a dream getaway for the comfortable." That should deeply affect how we feel about one another, with all our faults and inconvenient "noises." Remember in the Gospels when the disciples wanted to get away for a vacation with Jesus and instead five thousand hungry people showed up. "Send them away," the disciples complained. "No, you feed them and then clean up after them," was Jesus' response. Inconvenient? Sure, but selflessness takes care of inconvenience.

Christianity isn't about being comfy. We have been born again to serve selflessly so others can encounter the love of God. Church is to be a Holy Ghost hospital where life-giving effort is being poured out on all who come for help. So while we may desire a vacation getaway, God calls us to do the uncomfortable instead and put ourselves aside. We must see the world through His eyes. Now where did I put those new glasses?

An Old Way into the Woods

"Where were you when I laid the earth's foundation?"
(Job 38:4 NLT).

There was an old road in the town where I grew up. It was either an old cart path to the hay fields—dating back to the time when that part of New England was mostly farmland—or perhaps it was a long forgotten public way from before the time of automobiles. No matter its origin, it became to me a place of adventure. It wound its way deep into the woods—how far is what I was determined to discover. Every summer afternoon of my eleventh year I would head for the road's entrance at the back of old Mr. Goodmore's property line. Notebook in hand, I was determined to map the old pathway. Imagination was my companion. I charted markers—an old willow tree, a large white rock, and so on.

One day, after finding a side path that took me about 125 yards deeper into the trees, I discovered the remnants of an ancient stone wall. Still intact in places, it spoke of an earlier age. Someone had labored here and marked off boundary lines to establish ownership of the property—but who? I pictured a settler family, pilgrims most likely. We were not far from Plymouth Plantation. Were there second-generation Mayflower passengers who came here to carve out a new life in the new world? I searched for more signs of their existence.

The next day I found what I was looking for—an ancient foundation, barely visible under the leaves and underbrush. This had been somebody's dwelling place. There could be no doubt, the facts were clear—this had been home to someone long, long ago.

I never found the answer as to who lived there. Old Mr. Goodmore may have been able to tell me, but he passed away with cancer over one winter. With the passing of time I stopped my wondering visits. My eleventh year transitioned into teen years and the old road became just a cut through to a friend's house in the new development that had gone up so quickly in my fast-changing town.

Today, my way of adventure is a recreational road for motorcycles and four wheelers. I sometimes drive past and see them—high powered machines that travel speedily over the old ruts. I am certain my foundation is still hidden away from view. Nearly fifty seasons of falling leaves, my lifetime's years' worth of summer growth. Fifty winters, fifty warm spring times.

There are ancient pathways all around us. Few ever find them. We are too much in a hurry. We zoom along modern highways at great speed, never noticing the forests to our left and right. In my part of the country— if you are quick enough—you can often still see the aged stone walls along the thoroughfare, pointing back into the woods—back, back, to a different time. Adventure still calls.

It's the same in the spiritual realm. Jeremiah 6:16 reads, "This is what the Lord says: 'Stand at the crossroads and look; ask for the ancient paths, ask where the good way is, and walk in it, and you will find rest for your souls" (NIV). Ever feel like you "ought" to do something good or "ought not" to do something nefarious? We have that sense of "ought" in us because there exists an *original ought* and we are made in His image. Planned order in the cosmic chaos. An ancient way to be traveled that takes us within. There you will discover the old, old foundation. Someone laid a Cornerstone. He can bring order out of chaos in your life. With just a word, He will draw your boundary lines in pleasant places. Allow Him to establish ownership in you. This journey will become the greatest adventure of your life. Take it slowly. While others speed past, you will chart things that they will never see.

Disciple

"Jesus said to all of his followers, 'If you truly desire to be my disciple, you must disown your life completely, embrace my cross as your own, and surrender to my ways'" (Luke 9:23).

I have a problem with my email today; I am getting messages in—but my replies just sit in a queue in my outbox going nowhere. I don't know what the problem is, but I do know that the system is useless and stagnant this way. Communication is a two-way street—if it isn't, the process is pointless.

It reminds me of our walk with God. He fills us up daily with His word. He blesses us with abundant life. He pours out love from heavenly storehouses. But if it stops there, with the inbox only—well, you guessed it—we become stagnant. Remember, He fills us up to pour us out. We aren't consumers of Christianity; we are its purveyors.

I think I am beginning to get it, this idea of being a disciple. According to Jesus, there are three major aspects involved—denying myself, carrying a cross daily, and following Him. Luke 9:23 (KJ21) says, "If any man will come after Me, let him deny himself and take up his cross daily, and follow Me."

Denying myself can be tricky, but I have learned that this is rarely a dramatic result of an altar-call decision to "never be self-centered again!" No, denying oneself happens in everyday moments. It is simply not caving to selfishness—ten minutes at a time. This could mean allowing some driver to proceed through an intersection before we enter it. It could mean sitting at the lonely one's lunch table instead of with our buddies. Or maybe it requires asking a follow-up question and really listening

53

to the answer instead of bailing out of the conversation with an "I'm so very busy" excuse. Every ten minutes presents a new opportunity to be second—first.

Taking up our cross is the next step. We do not bear the weight of sin as Christians, but we do carry the weight of responsibility for having been purchased by Christ, "You are not your own; you were bought at a price." (1 Cor. 6:19b-20a NIV). The weight on the life of every true disciple is an understanding of the transaction that brought us forgiveness, and carrying the cross reminds us that we owe a debt of love to all. The one who is forgiven, loves—and there is no greater symbol of true love than the cross. So then, it is not an overpowering weight. Indeed, you never want to be apart from its life-changing power.

Following is last. We are not leaders. In truth, disciples are really good followers. We learn to put our feet in the Lord's sandal prints as He dances through this world. But wherever He leads, we take the cross with us. So that we view circumstance through the frame of the rough wood—each person in the strong shadow of love and forgiveness. What a joy to dance with Him and to embrace our world in the freedom of discipline. For that is just what disciples do.

Harvest

"This is what the Lord Almighty says: 'Now hear these words,
"Let your hands be strong so that the temple may be built."
This is also what the prophets said who were present when
the foundation was laid for the house of the Lord Almighty. ...
The seed will grow well, the vine will yield its fruit, the ground
will produce its crops, and the heavens will drop their dew'"
(Zechariah 8:9,12a NIV).

Establishing a place of true worship here on the planet has never been an easy task. Throughout history, God's people have struggled with idolatry, discouragement, invading enemies, you name it. But Scripture instructs us that God longs for our earnest devotion, and when we do truly draw near to Him, He responds by drawing near to us. As a church, it's His intimate presence that we seek. We must overcome the maddening momentum of this fading earth and diligently seek His face.

The book of Zechariah describes a time when the Lord's people were in the process of rebuilding the Temple. The work slowed, and distractions were numerous. However, they were not working alone! They had a heavenly support system in place. "For I am planting seeds of peace and prosperity among you," said the Lord of Hosts. Then the following rallying cry! "So don't be afraid. Be strong and get on with rebuilding the temple" (Zech. 8:12-13 NLT)!

Building a peaceful, loving, prosperous place of worship is a challenge. It is warfare! But there is no business more important to the Father's heart. He inhabits our praise! Heaven is, indeed, open. Divine seeds are being deposited amongst us. Let's labor until the harvest is ready.

I pulled into the drive through at the local donut shop one morning. It was my birthday, and (with Amanda's reluctant permission) I was planning to celebrate with my favorite, the coffee roll. A rare treat, the coffee roll—delicious, yet too big, scrumptious, full of calories! I could already taste it as I drove up to the microphone and waited.

"Can I help you?" asked the server. I happily placed my order for that big, fattening coffee roll.

After a pause came the dreaded reply, "I'm sorry, we are all out of coffee rolls this morning. Would you like something else?"

Crestfallen, I substituted. The surefire chocolate glazed crueler would be a solid choice.

"Out of those, too," said the voice from inside.

Substituting again, I asked for the always tasty blueberry donut.

"We don't carry those."

Now, I'm scrambling. A jelly stick? Chocolate frosted donut?

"Out...sold out... discontinued." It was comical.

By now, it was obvious that the server was feeling badly for me. "Would you like to try one of our fall harvest special donuts? I will give it to you free for your birthday." (Somewhere in the donut debacle I had let that bit of birthday information slip in.)

"Yes!" I replied. Prudence let out a whoop from her car seat, and Amanda just grinned, happy that the end was in sight.

I pulled around the corner and there, the smiling server handed me a bag—the fall harvest special. As I pulled away, Amanda announced, "She gave us three of them! Three donuts! A harvest indeed!" My single coffee roll request had multiplied and soon all three of us were munching on the generous supply of donut goodness—a happy family.

Sometimes, when we are denied that "coffee roll" we so *wanted*, we end up receiving a joyful exchange that blesses not only ourselves, but those around us. "Happy Birthday, son," said the true voice of my Father, who loves me wonderfully.

The Figure near the Fence

"Casting down imaginations, and every high thing that exalteth itself against the knowledge of God, and bringing into captivity every thought to the obedience of Christ"
(2 Corinthians 10:5 KJV).

I t had snowed all day the day before, but now it was calm. The streets had been plowed, the sidewalks cleared, and the steps sanded. As evening turned to nightfall, I called Tyler, my cocker spaniel, and grabbed his leash. "C'mon boy!" I summoned, "Let's go outside." Tyler needs no second call for a romp out of doors. He jumps and paws at the door before I can reach it, and once opened he bolts like lightning for the backyard. He loves the snow and his glee is evident as he leads the way, towing me behind. Tonight was no different—until suddenly, he stopped in his tracks.

A low rumble of a growl came from my usually happy pup. He took a step back, still growling. "What is it Tyler?" I asked as if expecting an answer. Through the deepening darkness he had sensed something. What was it?

We live on the edge of the forest and deer are plentiful. At night we often hear coyotes howling at the moon. Had one of these creatures ventured too close to home? I strained my eyes and stared into the gloaming. There was definitely a lone figure that I could barely make out, right there near the back fence! I stared, Tyler stared, but none of us moved—not dog, not man, not the intruder.

"Who's there?" I called out.

No answer came. The standoff continued.

A minute seemed an eternity. Tyler growled in earnest, and I must admit I was feeling sketchy. Why didn't the stranger move, make a sound—something? The more I stared, the creepier things got. I began to edge backward, not wanting to turn my back to the scene. Still no movement from the figure near the fence! Was he taunting us?

I took a few more backward steps, and then (yes, I admit it) I broke on a dead run for the porch, a little more spooked than I would like to own up to. Calling to Amanda, I exclaimed, "There's someone out there in the yard! He's just, well—standing there."

With a wry grin she looked back at me hovering behind her. "That would be the snowman I made with the kids this afternoon," she informed me. "I don't expect it to move much."

Sometimes, the things that frighten us are really harmless. Our imaginations carry us to heights beyond reason. We play out scenarios and confrontations in our head that we suppose might happen—but they are not reality. Reality is this—I am a child of God, and there is nothing the enemy can throw at me to harm me. There is no standoff needed. The Bible says plainly—resist the devil and he will flee.

The Prank

"You may be sure that your sin will find you out"
(Numbers 32:23 NLT).

I t had all the makings of a great summer.

I had accepted a position as a counselor on the staff of an overnight camp about twenty-five miles from my home. They were pretty desperate for help that year, so I was hired on sight. Sensing the adventure, a buddy of mine took the job of head chef in the camp kitchen. I was to be "staff" to the youth campers for the first four weeks of the season, then the teens took over for the second half of the summer. Not yet eighteen years old myself, I found out that teen campers presented a small problem. Basically, I was responsible to keep the lid on a few dozen of my contemporaries. Not having much leadership experience, I was flying by the seat of my pants. Like I said, it had all the makings of a great summer.

Our director wasn't very seasoned either. He wore a big cabana hat, drawstring under his chin. His sandals bore testimony of sheltered, cultured summers by revealing a tan line where his socks used to be. He had a lanyard with a whistle attached on a big silver ring, and he used it often. He referred to us as "chaps" and "laddies." The female staff were just as unfortunate, being labeled as "lasses." He was sincere, I'll give him that. He ran a tidy ship. Roll call was at 6:45 a.m. Calisthenics on the quad by 7 a.m. Breakfast at 7:20 (we got five minutes to wash up after morning stretch). The whole day ran like clockwork. It was enough to make a teenager feel uneasy—we chaps knew we had to throw Don the Director off kilter by summer's end. We made it our mission.

The real serious succession of pranks began with the arrival of teen camp. The campers were eager to participate in every joke we unveiled. There were the usual and predictable water balloons. We swapped out the director's toothpaste with—never mind. Itching powder and garlic gum were employed, phony wake up calls (complete with revelry at 3 a.m.) were pulled off routinely. We had, by now, officially made it our end of summer purpose to truly rattle our director. And thus, we conceived "the prank."

Director Don had a small sports car, a foreign two-seater, five-speed manual transmission motor car that he enjoyed driving up and down the dirt road that led to the camp entrance, usually at breakneck speeds. That car was a thing of beauty, and it was Don's first love. The prank seemed simple, yet brilliant—the goal was to place the beloved automobile onto the raft that was anchored in the lake. The night was chosen—it was to be Friday night before the final Saturday of teen camp. "What a way to end the summer," we cajoled. Little did we know.

The appointed day came. All afternoon during arts and crafts, we chaps exchanged knowing glances, acknowledging our hour of prank glory was soon to be. That evening after lights out (always 9:30 p.m. sharp), two of our best swimmers quietly untied the raft from its mooring and towed it in to shallow water where it was positioned at the end of the dock. It seemed easy enough—push the director's auto down the hill that led to the waterfront, out onto the narrow wooden wharf, and then on to the raft. From there it would be a simple process of letting nature take its course as the raft drifted about the lake. We waited until the light in Don's window was off and we were certain that he was asleep before roll call. As the coast was clear, we scampered up to the staff parking area. Don never locked the vehicle. "We're miles away from society, deep in the woods," he would say. "Who's gonna steal my car out here?" Little did he know!

We pushed the car silently to the edge of the parking lot and one of our teens from teen camp climbed in behind the wheel. With the stick shift in the neutral position, we got up some speed. The car rolled nicely as a group of six of us gave a final shove in the direction of the wharf. "Slow down!" we hissed.

"I don't know how," offered the frightened young lady in the driver's seat. We hadn't counted on this. She was stomping on the clutch pedal wondering why the brakes would not engage. The precious auto reached the wharf at about 25 miles per hour, and to her amazement—and ours— she managed to steer it the length of the structure. That is where "the great separation" took place. The raft, awaiting its cargo, was free-floating in the shallow water. Due to the darkness, we had not noticed the growing gap between raft and wharf. For a precarious moment the car rested with one foot in each kingdom, front wheels on the not-as-steady-as-one-might-think raft. The rear wheels stayed on the pier. For a minute that seemed like eternity, Don's beloved automobile performed a great feat of balancing until physics took over and the car nosedived into three feet of water. Our dampened driver climbed out the side window and ran for her cabin and into her bed, where she hoped that wet clothes and soggy sneakers would not give her "part of the prank" identity away. We chaps and laddies got busy trying to push the car, which was up to its gunnels in lake water, back onshore. It was a trying effort and we soon realized that it couldn't be done. So, despite the late hour, we summoned a tow truck and dragged the soggy sedan onto the beach. I guess you could say that it wasn't funny.

I learned a valuable life lesson that summer that has served well over my years as a pastor. Once you begin with a bad behavior, it builds up momentum and consequences are sure to occur. "Sin always takes you further than you wanted it to go," is how we say it at LifeHouse. For example, no one ever started out in life with the stated ambition of becoming addicted to alcohol or drugs. But somehow, the wheels get rolling, and that stop at the bottom isn't there or it just doesn't hold, and soon you're sunk. If that is your situation, I've got a good tow rope available.

No matter what mess you've gotten into, it can be forgiven. That's the message heaven offers us. It's why Jesus walked the planet. He will lead you out—one step at a time. He offers the only way out—step by step, one good choice at a time. It begins with confessing your faults. Just like we had to fetch Don out of bed and tell him what we had done on the night of the failed car on the raft prank. The steps are small and manageable at first (requiring only courage), but as the day breaks, things are seen more clearly in the light, and you begin to run.

Back at the camp, much to our amazement, the director's car started right up the next morning. It reportedly ran well for years afterward—no doubt a little worse for the wear. You'll be surprised by your new start as well. You still have plenty of life left in your motor—once you've dried it out for a while.

Changing Seasons

"God was delighted to give us birth by the truth of his infallible Word so that we would fulfill his chosen destiny for us and become the favorite ones out of all his creation" (James 1:18).

What is it about the first hint of spring that makes us hopeful, happy, eager for warm days to come? One Monday morning, I stepped outside and felt the warm breezes of spring, something I hadn't experienced for many weeks. I knew there was still winter to go through, but the promise was there. Days would be coming when the sun would feel warm on our faces and the earth would open up in bright colors. Gone would be the slate-gray skies of February and the white face of the ground under its snow cover. Green and gold will take their places. The Lord builds truth into the earth's seasons, wintry days to succumb to warmth—always.

Some of us are in the throes of an emotional winter; some feel the physical chill of poor health. Some face financial troubles that hold fast to us like ice on the tree limbs. We long to break free. Take a lesson from the warm breeze that came over the hills that Monday morning—seasons change in life! And there is hope offered by a loving Father who never changes. His love and loyalty to His children are constant.

The psalmist wrote, "The heavens declare the glory of God; the skies proclaim the work of his hands. Day after day they pour forth speech; night after night they reveal knowledge." (Psalm 19:1-2a NIV). I am certain the word that came flowing from the warming blue sky the start of that February morning was *hope*! It is my hope that a new season of encouragement will be yours today. Try something new, break a bad habit, turn over a new leaf, pray more often, send a note, stretch your wings, read some chapters, laugh.

Speaking of laughter, I always enjoy telling the story of my "new" station wagon that was given to me many years ago by some well-meaning friends. Although it ran okay, it looked for all the world like it was ready to fall apart. If things look like they're falling apart for you, remember what James 1:18 states—that we are His prized possession on display for all of creation to view. "Here is one who belongs to Me," the Lord can say. What does the world see at that moment? Do we look like my station wagon—ready to come apart at the seams? Or have we taken on the responsibility of nailing our old selves to the cross and allowing the life of Christ to shine through us? I've noticed that when He becomes more visible, we see ourselves in a better light.

In the next few verses (1:19–25), James tells us, in short, what a child of God looks like.

A. **Quick to listen.** Do we surround ourselves with noble truth, or are our ears filled with the things of this world? Do we obey the King with pleasure, realizing His commandments are life-giving—or do we tune in for a few minutes on Sunday out of a sense of duty? We do have authority over our lives, and it is our responsibility to learn what pleases Him. A soldier who doesn't listen to his/her commanding officer is going to be in trouble.

B. **Slow to speak.** Intake must exceed outgo! If you want to hear from God, listen more and talk less. Many of us learned to pray by listing off a bunch of needs and desires—we weren't taught to listen. It only makes sense that a proper view of God would include the notion that He has a lot more to offer than we do.

C. **Slow to get angry.** Anger is an emotion, and many of us are controlled by our emotions. Instead, we are to be under the control of the Holy Spirit. Have you ever tried to talk to an angry person? Do they listen? Not really. Are they slow to speak? Rarely.

Don't just listen to the Word—do what it says. That's what James tells us. It is the season to get things right.

Family

"We are all vitally joined to one another, with each contributing to the others" (Romans 12:5).

I had another cute "Prudence moment" happen yesterday—and as usual, it taught me a life lesson. We were talking about our family, and I asked her, "Prudence, what's the best thing about our family?"

The answer came as a surprise as she pointed to me and said, "You!"

Caught a little off guard, I responded, "Well, what makes Daddy the best thing about our family?"

Without missing a beat, she said, "Mama." Pretty good insight for a youngster, wouldn't you say?

It's true though—our family relationships should help us to make one another better. And when we allow the Holy Spirit's control to overtake our "selves," we function as conduits of divine influence. I was reading in Daniel the other day, the familiar story of the three Hebrew lads and the fiery furnace. How much strength did they gain for having stood up to that trial together? If it had been Shadrach alone, without Meshach and Abednego, would he have stood strong? "A cord of three strands is not quickly broken," Scripture says (Eccles. 4:12 NIV). If they had not been bound and tied, I'll reckon those three men would've been holding hands as they were thrust into the flames.

I was exiting the kitchen area at church one recent Sunday. It was after the morning service, and the coffee line was crowded around the doorway. Not as nimble as I once was (was I ever nimble?), I zigged when I meant to zag—and I was momentarily off balance. One of the ladies immediately sprang into action and got prepped to catch me as I fell. I regained my balance, however, as well as my composure, and the tumble was averted. Still, the would-be catcher stayed braced, arms extended, until she was certain I was making forward progress and under my own steam.

What a picture of church life! We should always be aware of who is in the crowd, about to fall—and we should be poised and ready to catch them. Even if we are just "available if needed," it will mean much to someone who may be just a bit out of kilter. One of the lessons the Lord has taught me through Parkinson's is the ability to accept help. I have need of assistance from time to time with small things or in larger tasks. I needed help putting my keys on my keychain and a dear sister took care of the problem. I had a broken piece of furniture and a dear brother came and repaired it. You see, we aren't independent of one another. A family helps each other out. The Christian faith is really not a personal thing at all. Paul writes that we are members of one another. Considering how many "one anothers" there are in the New Testament, it should cause us to pick up on the emphasis of Scripture. Our faith is a group effort.

Jude verse 24 says our God is able to keep us from falling. Isn't it nice to know that He lets us—His saints—lend a helping hand in the process? Be poised and ready—somewhere someone is zigging, not zagging. They may need a little help to stand steady.

Carols

"For you know the grace of our Lord Jesus Christ,
that though he was rich, yet for your sake he became poor,
so that you through his poverty might become rich"
(2 Corinthians 8:9 NIV).

The Christmas season is always very special. Growing up, I can recall Christmas caroling with members of my home church. The familiar carols were like dear friends you see but once a year. We sang them in harmonies, our voices following the parts and paths that we recalled from earlier times. We would pack ourselves into a caravan of cars and make the rounds, unpacking ourselves at each stop and stomping our boots to ward off the cold. The town hall, the nursing home, the houses near the projects—we would begin at nightfall and carol until the neighborhood homes turned off their lights.

Leo and Mary were always our last stop. The elderly couple lived in a trailer just big enough for the two of them. Mary was a thin, tiny woman—somewhere in her senior years. Leo was a double amputee and would sit in his old wheelchair that squeaked and groaned. Mary would always greet us at the kitchen door, nodding her head as she counted. "You have more carolers than last Christmas!" she would say. "Let's see if we are going to fit!" With that, we would all pile into the warm kitchen, packed side by side around the table that held a small silver tinsel Christmas tree and two well-used coffee mugs. "Let me get Leo," she would cluck. "Leo! Christmas is here!"

I suppose we were Christmas to Leo and Mary. She would wheel her dear husband to the edge of our well-bundled circle, and there they would listen as we sang the good news. And sing we did. Like the angels on that first Christmas night, we filled the little home with the best we had. Before the first verse of the first song was completed, old Leo would always grab his cloth handkerchief from his pocket and hold it to his face while his shoulders shook in sobs that he could not control. Mary would fuss over him a bit, "Are you okay, dear?" she would ask her husband. "He's just very happy," she would explain to us.

"Happy," I would muse, looking again at the tiny table and imagining the mornings of toast and marmalade they would share. I wondered what they spoke about over their instant coffee served in the worn mugs. They had next to nothing—just each other, really. But they had found that to be enough. Singing now, in that poor but contented home, we felt a sense of awe fall over us, and suddenly we were that angel choir—invading poverty and pain, not unlike that first Christmas night. Our voices swelled, choked with emotion as tears dropped on to our carol booklets. The words of the old songs came alive in our hearts—Emmanuel, God is with us.

As I looked around the humble home, I considered the Son of Man stepping out of heaven, entering a tiny stable—coming to win our hearts with love. He stooped low so that all could reach—and somehow on this night He had come again to a tiny trailer as our own hearts welcomed Him.

Nowadays, I love the Christmas season at LifeHouse. We hold a special Christmas Eve service each year, complete with soft lights and sacred songs. And to this day, as our voices rise and sing of one silent night so many years ago, I journey to Christmases past and behold the faces of old friends gathered in a cozy kitchen, lifting their voices in earnest jubilation. If I listen carefully, I can still hear dear old Mary calling, "Leo! Christmas is here!"

Trust

"Trust in the Lord completely, and do not rely on your own opinions. With all your heart rely on him to guide you and he will lead you in every decision you make" (Proverbs 3:5).

Trust—it's hard to come by in our present world. Not long ago, the planet was less traversed and, for the most part, more trustworthy. People were more connected. Generations of families lived under the same roof. They shared meals. TV did not dominate the dinner hour—conversation did. The pace was slower. Not so, now. It's not uncommon in our current age for the average family breadwinner to have an hour commute each day to and from the office. The highways are packed morning and night—and traffic reporting is seemingly a part of every radio station's format. Autos, autos everywhere. Meals are grabbed on the fly—fast food isn't always fast enough for our liking. The family dinner table is a memory. We text—not talk. We eat behind the wheel.

Now, the automobile has been around for a long time—but when we consider all of human history, it shows up on the grid as a "recent invention." Up until the early years of the twentieth century, automobile travel was non-existent (hadn't been invented yet). Eventually it became somewhat available, but unreliable—and frankly, rare. People just didn't travel as they now do. They worked in the neighborhoods where they lived. They knew people. The paperboy was the son of so and so (*"Can you believe he's getting so big? Going to high school next year!"*). The milk and eggs came from the dairy farm across town (*glass bottles in the milk box on your porch*), and the hardware store was operated by Mr. Smith who went to grade school with us. (*"How's it going, Smitty? How's the wife? Got to pick up some nails this morning, let's have a look.*") Point being, no one drove a great distance to work far from home—people stayed local and roots were deeper. Trust came with the territory. Neighborhoods were filled with neighbors—not hoods.

In the changeover to the fast-paced society that we now know, cynicism has replaced trust like the car replaced the horse and buggy. Roadways are clogged with strangers traveling at high rates of speed—or, worse yet, at a crawl. Commuter railways are packed with unknown and yet familiar, regular travelers who routinely isolate from one another—headphones in and suspicions high. Few things have escaped this transition. The local paper can be accessed on your personal computer. Your milk is stacked in the cooler at the huge grocery store the next town over—and if you're completely honest, you'll admit that you don't know where it originally came from. Big box stores have taken over the hardware business—open late so you can still get in and out after your evening commute.

A friend of mine was asked to speak to a group of pastors a few years ago. He gave them all a piece of paper and a pen, along with these instructions: write the names of your closest neighbors—to your north, south, east, and west. Then write the name of a widow and orphan who is receiving ministry from you personally. Jesus said that loving our neighbor was a requirement for belonging to His kingdom. Taking care of widows and orphans is considered "pure religion that God accepts" according to the New Testament. Well, the pastors with the papers drew blanks across the board. No one could successfully name four neighbors, never mind a widow or an orphan. My friend was never asked to speak to the group again.

With the world getting less and less "neighborly" and with trust taking a back seat to cynical skepticism, it causes one to search for a root system that can hold. Our foundation is only as strong as our circumstances allow. Good day—we're okay. Bad day—it seems everything is up for grabs. We become less caring as individuals. We sink into anonymity and figure it is the only way to survive. However, we are strangely unsteady. We must admit that we are lost and alone, and there we will stay—unless there is an unchanging absolute with which we can connect. A compass. A map. A defining principle. Something higher.

Enter the Bible.

Having been in Christian work for some thirty years, I have gained enormous trust in the Bible. I believe it is inspired and true. I have never seen it fail. But I must admit that it can be confusing. Many who consider themselves Christians don't know where to begin reading their Bible—and much of it seems intimidating. But in truth, its sixty-six individual books come together nicely and have an order to them that allows for easy understanding. Once we understand where things fit, it should clear the way for some effective action.

How we conduct our lives is a direct line to our trust in God's Word. After all, it was Jesus who told us the parable of the wise man and the foolish man. One built on rock, the other on sand. We all know this story, but I have yet to see anybody—young or old—tell me what made the difference between the two foundations. What caused one to be shaky and the other rock solid? It's a trust issue, clear as can be.

In Matthew chapter 7 where the story is found, Jesus tells us that if we hear His words and put them into practice, it is like building upon a solid foundation for your life. On the other hand, the one who hears His words and does not put them into practice is like someone who builds their life on shifting sand. Shifting sand won't hold roots. And that makes the difference—having an authority to direct you will keep you from tumbling under life's circumstances. And something else—it also will put you into a family relationship with other believers. In other words, it creates a new kind of neighborhood where caring, understanding, and love prevail. This is a key concept.

You see, Christianity was never intended to be a personal thing. It's a group effort. God knew that human beings function best with help from others. At creation, God initially pronounced all things "good" until He saw Adam's aloneness. For the first time, He uttered the phrase, "That's not good." And so He created a family. He later walked and talked with those He created—Adam and Eve, then Enoch and Noah. He started that family with Abraham.

In the New Testament, Jesus called together a group of disciples and taught them to pray "Our Father" *not* "My Father." Note the language of that prayer, the one we call the Lord's Prayer. "Give *us*," "forgive *us*," and "lead *us*." It's *us,* not *me*. We are responsible to and for one another, according to God's plan. If you are out there on your own, you are missing the "us" that is so necessary to the life of faith.

It's time to trust. You won't be stepping out on a limb. Instead, you'll be taking your place in the family tree.

Understanding the Map

"Truth's shining light guides me in my choices and
decisions; the revelation of your Word makes my pathway
clear" (Psalms 119:105).

The Bible can be an intimidating read. In fact, if you are a new Christian you may have absolutely no idea where to begin reading. I have heard that many people are referred to the gospel of John for their first crack at the pages. In response to that, I will often reach for a copy of a great literary masterpiece. "Start in the middle," I'll say, "anywhere." But how will the reader know the storyline or the plot development if they jump in midstream? The characters will be strangers. The book will seem daunting. It's the same with the Bible. It has an order and a plot that must be recognized in order to benefit fully from its pages of truth. So to that end, we will follow a simple formula that will bring us to more revelation from Scripture, resulting in proper action. If we understand, we can better trust. If we trust, we can act accordingly. So here is the formula: Begin at the beginning.

Genesis is the first book in our Bible. The title means "origins." It is a book of firsts. It details creation and the flood. It tells how sin entered the human race. It records the first birth (Cain) and the first murder (Abel). The first mention of the word *love* is found in Genesis 22, with the story of Abraham offering his beloved son, Isaac, on the altar.

Genesis gives us world history as mankind branches out to fill the earth. Yet in chapter 12, you'll notice the book takes a sharp turn. With the call of Abraham—from whom God will form a nation—the Bible moves from general world history to the storyline of one people, the Jews.

Abraham is the patriarch of the family of God on planet earth. Genesis 12:1–3 records a promise made and a nation formed. The rest of the Bible becomes the story of that one nation. Even in the New Testament we are told that believers are grafted in to the tree which is Israel. God also promises Abraham a homeland. His nation will live in a secure environment—the Promised Land.

However, as Genesis comes to a close the nation of Israel is not in the Promised Land—they are in Egypt. The last word in the book of Genesis is (look it up) "Egypt," and the next book in your Bible (naturally called Exodus, meaning to exit) tells all about how the Jews miraculously exited Egypt. To escape the slavery and oppression of Egypt, a hero named Moses steps into the limelight and delivers the Jewish nation out of Pharaoh's iron hand.

Exodus chronicles the escape from Egyptian slavery and follows the Jewish nation into their wilderness-wandering. It describes the law being given in the form of Ten Commandments. While dwelling in the wilderness, Moses receives instructions to build a tent-like tabernacle to house the worship of God's people. Upon completion, Moses tries to enter the tabernacle, but the presence of the Lord is so thick and overpowering that he cannot go in. He needs a method of access—a ticket, an invitation to approach.

Interestingly, the next book of the Bible's name in Hebrew means "the way of approach," and it covers (among other things) the needed information to enter God's presence—a sacrifice must be made. The book begins with instruction about the sacrificial system. We call the book Leviticus.

Sacrifice. After Adam and Eve committed the first act of sin on the planet, they hid themselves from the Lord. It's beautiful to see that Deity came searching for the fallen couple. Upon finding them, He took the life of an animal (the first death on planet earth was a sacrifice) and covered the shame of Adam and Eve. This is where the concept of a substitute death was introduced. This is why Cain's offering was later rejected by the Lord as he had brought forth the fruit of the ground. It was turned away. No death. No blood. His brother, Abel, brought a lamb and slew it.

74

It was accepted. The pattern had been set by the Lord Himself absolving the first sin and sinners.

The book of Numbers follows Leviticus, and to no surprise Israel takes a census. *Deuteronomy* means the second law, and in its pages we find the Ten Commandments repeated along with other rules and regulations. When God wants to emphasize a truth, repetition is often the way. All the while, the Jews are still wandering in the wilderness. At the end of the book we say goodbye to Moses, who passes away before he can enter the beloved Promised Land. Their leader was dead, so they would need someone else to take command. Enter Joshua. Interestingly, that is the next book of Scripture—the book of Joshua. After Joshua's passing, the Jews remain leaderless for a time, and they are governed by a group of chieftains called "judges." And that is our next book in the Bible—Judges.

During the time of the judges a woman named Ruth came on the scene—and her story is chronicled for us in the book that bears her name. A primary reason her story is recorded in the Word of God is summed up in the last word of the book. Ruth closes with the name David—Ruth's descendant and the future king.

One of the most prominent judges was a man named Samuel. He had the distinction of crowning the first two kings of Israel. The wrong king (the people's choice) was named Saul, and we are introduced to him in 1 Samuel. Then we meet God's choice for king of Israel in 2 Samuel when we read of David and his actions as king. Following that, we have a listing or a history of the various kings who reigned on the throne of Israel. We find them, naturally, in the books of 1 and 2 Kings. Even more of their exploits are described in 1 and 2 Chronicles—the recording of the life and times of Israel's kings. There were good regimes and bad regimes—most were bad. Finally, 2 Chronicles closes with the children of Israel exiled in Babylon as discipline for their disobedience. There they stayed until a Jewish hero named Ezra began calling them home. Nehemiah organized the rebuilding of Jerusalem upon their return. Esther tells an amazing story of how the Jews escaped extermination while in exile. And there you have the books in order—Ezra, Nehemiah, and Esther.

Job, Psalms, and Proverbs, along with Ecclesiastes, are literary works that the Jewish nation preserved while in captivity. Job, the oldest book in the Bible, reads like a movie script. Psalms serves as a Jewish hymnbook written mainly by King David, while Proverbs and Ecclesiastes follow as Solomon's literary contribution. Add his love song, Song of Songs, and we reach a milestone in our Bible. From here on out, we have the prophets, who look ahead into the future and forecast the coming reign of the Messiah. From Isaiah to Malachi, major prophets and minor prophets bring us to the quiet that lies between the testaments, old and new. "He's coming!" they say.

Then, with the four Gospels the cry changes to "He's here!" And the story of Jesus is given—His life, His miracles, His death and resurrection, all written for us to read and believe. The book of Acts points back and says, "That was Him!" while the letters, or epistles, tell us how to conduct our lives as believers in the Messiah. From Romans to 3 John we have teaching and training for how to conduct church, family, and our personal lives. A little book called Jude and a climatic book entitled Revelation tell us "He's coming back again."

So, there you have it in simple form—the Bible outlined. Not so difficult. Now trust it, don't adjust it. Trust it; it has transcended the ages—and it will do the same for ages to come.

Cousin Barry—and Harry

"For when you saw me hungry, you fed me. When you found me thirsty, you gave me something to drink. When I had no place to stay, you invited me in" (Matthew 25:35).

When it all comes down to it, love is often expressed in the smallest of actions. The changing of a diaper, the morning cup of coffee, the dishes done. Jesus didn't set the bar too high—a cup of cold water would not be overlooked in the kingdom of heaven. One such action is etched deeply in my heart.

It was many years ago now when I was a freshman in college. Away from home for the first time, I found the party lifestyle to be inviting. One night I went to a club with a handful of buddies, and there I stayed until the wee hours of the morning. I made it back to my dorm just before dawn and crashed into my bunk. I had only been asleep for a few minutes when my RA knocked on my door. "Loren, let's go for a walk," he said. Figuring I was in some sort of trouble, I obliged, and we strolled out toward the highway. On the overpass, there was a walking bridge and the two of us stopped there.

"Your parents tried to reach you by phone all night long. Where were you?" I wasn't proud of my answer. I knew something serious was at hand. "Your cousin Barry was killed in an automobile accident yesterday afternoon. They're on their way to pick you up and bring you home."

My shock became tears, and the tears just wouldn't stop. I walked on alone. Barry—my cousin and my friend! He was such a part of my life and I could not imagine life without him. I stumbled up the stairs to my dorm, packed a few things into a duffle bag, and climbed into my parent's waiting car just a few minutes later. The drive home was filled with a million questions—how did this happen? How is his family taking it? When is the funeral?

The next few days were a blur. The funeral came and went. The youth group at our home church was devastated. I walked through the experience like some kind of zombie. However, the following Monday it was time to return to school. I had been gone for about a week.

Back on campus, it suddenly hit me that I had totally forgotten to let the head of food services know that I was going to be away. I worked in the dish room, washing and stacking dishes for the school cafeteria. I had missed every shift that week and never called in an explanation. I expected to be fired as I entered the boss's office.

"There's no problem here," he said. "You covered every shift. Here's your paycheck."

"But, how?" I asked.

"Your friend Harry came down last week and got a copy of your schedule, and he personally worked each shift, punching your time card in the process."

I was speechless.

Later, Harry wouldn't talk about it. He just shrugged and smiled. "You okay?" he asked.

"I am," I answered. And I was—now.

What simple act of love can you accomplish today? It really doesn't have to be a grand affair; even a four-hour shift in the dish room may be remembered for a lifetime.

Dad's Last Smile

"Your lives light up the world. Let others see your light from a distance, for how can you hide a city that stands on a hilltop?"
(Matthew 5:14).

During creation, God made two great lights to hang in our sky—one is the source of daylight, the sun; the other glows from the reflection of the sun's light. You'll notice that the moon, or reflecting light, shines in the darkness. God has provided us with a perfect metaphor. He shines, we reflect. So in our own everyday routine we are necessarily reminded of the inescapable truth that there is True Light. And with our faces turned toward Him, we will reflect His pure light into the surrounding darkness.

My dad was a pastor for many years. Known for his sense of humor (mostly corny jokes), he had a smile a mile wide that he always wore upon his face. Rarely did I see that smile fade, no matter what the difficulty or circumstance. Late in life, however, he was diagnosed with Parkinson's disease, and his normally joyful features began to fade. During the last year of his life he was virtually expressionless—that is, until the night he passed away.

I sat by his bedside quoting Scripture and doing my best to sing the songs he loved. In the wee hours of the morning, I knew that he was expiring and that any of these gasping breaths would be his last. When it did come, I watched in amazement as a huge smile broke over his stony face, and right before my eyes I saw fifty years melt away! The faith that had carried him through life was now coming to fruition through death. It was Dad's best moment to reflect the glory of God—the light! But it's more than just facial expressions; Ephesians 5:1-2 says to "imitate God" by walking in love. Imagine that? We are called to have God-like character and to reflect that nature to each other—indeed, to everyone we meet.

A wise person once wrote that alongside the narrow road to heaven are found the discarded burdens that people leave behind as they journey closer to the throne. Early in the journey the items are small—a TV show, a pack of cards. But as the path winds on, the things left behind grow larger and larger and more significant—unhealthy relationships, addictions. None seem worthy to carry anymore, not this close to Love.

Walk on, Church, we are to be a city shining on a hill. We are the light of the world—but we are reflectors! We cannot serve two masters, we can only reflect one. We have made our choice—and He is Jesus.

By the way, Dad, thanks for doing it right.

Thoughts While Exercising

"The way I love you is like the way a servant wants to please his master, the way a maid waits for the orders of her mistress. We look to you, our God, with passionate longing to please you and discover more of your mercy and grace" (Psalms 123:2).

Okay, video disc in, and class begins. Onto the TV screen comes this guy—and he is a fitness expert. He knows all the moves, all the steps. We, on the other hand, watch intently, trying to mimic his every turn, twist, or jump (it gets a little funny). He does each move perfectly and encourages us that "we can do this." At least we're moving and sweating—that's got to be good, right? All the while, we keep our eyes glued to the screen, accepting each command and trying to implement it to the best of our ability.

Now, fast forward and it's the middle of the night, and I find myself awake and listening for that still, small voice. Turns out that He is interested in another form of lesson.

"You know how you kept your eyes on the exercise video—following the instructor's lead?"

"Yes," I reply.

"Well…that's how it is to be with Me. Follow My lead. I know the steps you should make and I will show them to you."

One of my favorite Scriptures is found in Psalm 123 and it says (paraphrased), "Like a servant to his master, like a maid to her lady's hand, so are our eyes fixed on you, Lord." In other words, we keep our eyes glued on Christ—awaiting His next signal for action.

The story is told (most say it's a true story) of a janitor at the World Trade Center in New York City. On September 11, 2001 he had been working there for years. Needless to say, he knew the buildings inside and out.

When the horror began unfolding on that fateful morning, he knew just what to do. First, he personally carried or escorted fifteen people down the fire stairs to safety. At ground level, he met the firefighters who were just responding, and with his master set of keys led them up inside to the spreading devastation. Then he began leading people out, dozens at a time, saying, "Follow me—I know the way." One look at his key ring was enough for many people to trust him. They followed him through the billowing smoke and found their way to safe ground. Trip after trip, the brave custodian went up and down those stairs—saving hundreds of lives in the process. His last trip down nearly cost him his life as he had to dive under a truck to escape the falling debris.

Some never followed the humble janitor that day. Distrust, dismay, fear, or bad advice kept many from leaving their places within the burning towers. According to the book of James in the Bible, the children of God are "quick to listen." The Word of the Lord is sure—it is a lamp to our feet. To follow the humble Savior is to find life itself. Many cower in fear or distrust—seemingly frozen in place. But, yes, you guessed it—the One who calls us out of darkness holds the keys. He knows the way through this life and to the next. He is God, after all. It only makes sense that we should listen to His voice above our own. What has He told you about this day?

Our job is to watch intently as our faith gets a workout lesson; we are to keep our eyes fixed on Jesus, the Author and Finisher of our faith (see Heb. 12:2). Remember, that faith is *not* dreamy wishes and hopes. No, faith is the substance of what we hope for—the evidence of what we believe. You can see evidence. Substance is—well, substantial. You can feel it. Faith without these "works" doesn't count as anything.

So (get the picture) our lives are to be lived like a fitness class—with our eyes glued on the Instructor, who calls out, "You can do it!" as we watch and wait for this Expert Teacher to dictate our next step. It won't be as perfect as His—but the trick is to keep moving, eyes fixed.

Angel in Harvard Square

"And show hospitality to strangers, for they may be angels from God showing up as your guests" (Hebrews 13:2).

I don't often see angels, but I know them when I do. We had one visit church one Sunday a number of years ago. I was preaching through the book of James in the New Testament, and the messages were hitting home for all of us. The verses about caring for the poor and ministering to orphans and widows penetrated our hearts. At the close of one particularly moving service, I walked off the platform and made my way to the rear of the sanctuary to pronounce the benediction. I prayed aloud and as soon as I said the "amen," I opened my eyes. There at the very front of the church stood a man facing the altar—his clothes were ragged and torn, and the dirt covering his body suggested he had spent many days without a roof over his head. How did he get there? He would have walked right by me on his way to the altar—but I had heard and seen nothing. A careful check of the congregation later proved the same—no one had seen or heard him enter the room.

I watched as the church sprang into action. It was the book of James come to life! Dollar bills and fast food coupons were handed to our visitor. Within the hour, he was soaking in one of the deacon's bathtubs. He said his name was Carlos. We got Carlos a place to stay for the night in a local shelter, promising him a good breakfast the next morning—but when I went to pick him up the next day, he was gone. The shopping cart with his belongings was no longer at the church where we had left it—he had vanished without a trace. I will always believe that Carlos was an angel— sent to test our faith and our commitment to living the Scripture.

I hadn't always entertained the angels so well. I was walking through Harvard Square in Cambridge, Massachusetts on a drizzly, cold November day. Head down against the wind and freezing rain, I heard him before I saw him. Begging for a handout was a young man, a foot taller than anyone around him, shirtless and shoeless, arms extended, pleading to the crowd. Digging into my pockets, I was caught short by my traveling partner who shut me down with, "He's an addict; don't support his bad habit." Slightly embarrassed, I walked past the young man, but just a few strides beyond I stopped and turned around. Everything was the same—the man at the newsstand, the taxi on the corner—but no tall young man without a shirt. I looked up and down the street—but there was no sign of him. I looked at the crumpled bill I had taken from my pocket, knowing I had missed an angel—unaware. I vowed never to miss another.

One night, back when I was a member of a different church, I was attending a church business meeting. There was heated discussion on some rather trivial topic. Trying to reach a consensus for a vote, the pros and cons were being voiced with passion. It was getting late, and yet the meeting labored on.

Much to everyone's surprise, a knock was heard at the door. A disturbed deacon opened the door to find a homeless man asking for a place to stay. The deacon explained that we were very busy with our business meeting and that the office would be open the next day—and the man was sent away. I distinctly heard the Father's voice as He asked, "Business meeting? The man at the door was your business."

God wants us to be useful for His kingdom at every moment. Sometimes He sends angels so that we can put our faith into practice. When you know it's God tugging at your heart, make sure you respond. Remember, His ways are higher than our ways, so when He asks you to do something that may not seem logical, be quick to recognize that something supernatural may be happening.

I have a dear friend who says, "If God asks you to quote John 3:16 out loud in the aisle of a supermarket, you can be sure there's someone in the next aisle praying desperately, 'Oh God, if You're real, make Yourself known to me.'" It may not be an angel this time, but then again, you never know!

The Blanket We Call Church

"Lord, you are my secret Hiding Place, protecting me from these troubles, surrounding me with songs of gladness!"
(Psalms 32:7a).

July 4th is the highlight of almost every summer. Cookouts, swimming, fireworks—it's a wonderful time of year.

Several years ago we took our young daughter, Prudence, to her first fireworks display. We pushed her stroller through the massive crowd, found a spot near Grandma Perry on the grass, and spread out our old blanket. After a short wait, darkness fell and the festivities began. At first, the fireworks display was a colorful exhibition of pops, sparkles, and flashes. Small stuff. Prudence was mesmerized. Soon, though, the night sky became a huge wash of fiery glow that ended with that familiar thunderous "boom" that echoed through the atmosphere (and my little girl's chest, no doubt). Prudence immediately put up both hands, turned to her parents and said, emphatically, "All done!"

Well, of course the fireworks were far from "all done." In fact, they were just beginning. There was nowhere to escape to, as the car was a great distance away in some municipal parking lot. So, Prudence took it upon herself to crawl under the blanket—putting her little hands over her ears. Whenever we peeked under to check on her, she would open one eye and say, "Hiding." And there she fell asleep—just like that.

Sometimes we all feel like hiding from the chaos that breaks around the world in mass demonstrations, earthquakes, and wild weather. We are reminded that an end is coming and wonder if we are getting close to seeing antichrist arrive on the scene. Meanwhile, the world is a chronic tinderbox, and the language of the New Age welcome is already included in bestsellers. Some have gone so far as to change the truth of the cross and the atonement for sin to "at-one-ment," calling for universal consciousness and an awakening to the deity of mankind. This redoubles my desire to be a church of the truth founded in Scripture. We will be people of the Word led by the Holy Spirit, not the spirit of antichrist that is at work *in* the world. Be sober, be vigilant, be sure. Sin separates us from God. The only road back to Life goes through an old rugged cross. There is peace and safety from the chaos under the blood of Christ.

Later that same night after the fireworks, I carried Prudence in from the car, still sleeping peacefully. I thought, *I don't know what is blowing up around you—sometimes it's the very things that seemed to sparkle and mesmerize, initially—but I do know that the Father has a big blanket you can crawl under and hide there until the chaos passes.*

It doesn't always end when we want it all to be "all done," but it passes. And remember, there are plenty of family members around to check up on you—to make sure you're peaceful through the trouble. We call that church.

From a Great Height

"And I will make them and the places all around my hill a
blessing, and I will send down the showers in their season; they
shall be showers of blessing" (Ezekiel 34:26 ESV).

One Monday morning the weather was phenomenal—bright, sunny, and warm. The Decker family decided that a walk along the Cape Cod Canal was in order—so we packed a lunch, grabbed the dog, and headed east. Along the way with the tunes boosted on the car stereo and the roads free of traffic, we were a happy bunch indeed.

We walked the canal road about an hour later. Prudence wanted a turn to hold the dog's leash, "By herself." (I wasn't certain who was walking whom, but they scurried along nonetheless.) When we reached the Sagamore Bridge we sat in the shade and cooled our collective heels for a bit. That was when we heard the voices overhead. Taken by surprise, we looked up to discover there were workers high above on the bridge's steel girders—calling back and forth to each other. And it soon became apparent that one of them was hollering down—to us!

"I'm going to be throwing down some things!" he shouted, his voice reaching us over the breeze. "I just didn't want you to worry!"

"Aren't you worried being up so high?" I called back.

"Naw, I'm used to it," came the reply.

A minute or so later, down came a small piece of equipment, landing twenty yards or so to our right. We smiled and waved, happy to be experiencing a "not your everyday occurrence." A tugboat and barge chugged past, seagulls dropped by for a visit, and we gave the dog some water. The afternoon lazed on—then "WUMP!" another delivery from on high came crashing down. Evangeline screamed; the rest of us looked startled. You see, in just that short period of time we had forgotten about the message from on high, "I'm going to be throwing down some things." As a result, we were totally surprised when the second package fell to the earth.

Okay—the application. God has blessing in store for us from on high, He promises to send it down to us. "Don't worry," He tells us. But we get so easily caught up in the details of each day that we tend to forget the message. We even act shocked when supply from above is dropped down to us.

Look up today. There is One calling, "I am sending some things down!" And they're coming your way. I pray that *all* your needs will be met in Christ.

We walked back to the van, a happy bunch—living the adventure.

Raccoon Story

"Be alert and of sober mind. Your enemy the devil prowls around like a roaring lion looking for someone to devour"
(1 Peter 5:8).

I love to tell my children bedtime stories. It's such a privilege to care for these little ones and to put a peaceful ending on their day. The tender years of stories at bedtime fly quickly by. They are gone before you know it. Over the years, each of my children has had a favorite story—and they would be requested often with no little amount of bouncing up and down and excited exclamations of delight.

The raccoon story has established itself as a top choice for more than one of my children. I have told it so many times, but I will now share it again for you—the enduring (not so endearing) raccoon story.

I was a care-free teenager, and it was summertime. Our friend from church youth group, Dale, had moved into her first apartment across town. She was a few years older than me and she had a fine stereo system, so, naturally, one Saturday afternoon I found myself headed for the new digs, record albums under my arm and friends Ron and Tina in tow. We were all set for a glorious afternoon of doing nothing—together.

Around mid-afternoon we heard a scratching sound at the door. Curious, I looked out the window. "Hey!" I hollered, "There's a raccoon outside on the deck with a red ribbon around its neck." Even more curious, I opened the door and stood next to the animal. He made several raccoon noises and then came closer to me. I reached down to pat him (or her) and to my surprise the raccoon obliged.

I stood up to call my buddies out to witness this close encounter with nature—but my sudden action startled the poor raccoon and it jumped high and bit me on the wrist. I quickly opened the door to the apartment and ran inside. Whether the nervous raccoon wanted another bite or he was fired up by the taste of blood, I don't know. What I did know was that I wanted to get to the hospital, because in my mind I was thinking "rabies," and the formerly tame raccoon was thinking, "I'm coming in!"

Into the apartment I ran with the big raccoon right on my heels. The girls screamed. Ron grabbed a broom and adopted a fencing stance in order to keep the animal at bay. Mr. Raccoon seemed unimpressed by Ron's noble jousting effort and subsequently ripped into the sofa and then dashed into the kitchen. I tried to shoo the beast toward the door—to no avail. His once endearing raccoon noises were now hisses and growls.

Waving towels only made the cornered animal more unsettled as he ran past our feeble defensive line and into the bedroom where he tried to climb the curtains. They came down along with the saucy animal. For a moment, the raccoon was ensnared in the fallen curtain. Ron had a moment of clarity amid the chaos and shut the bedroom door. We then herded the two hysterical girls into the bathroom and shut that door.

"I'm taking Loren to the ER," managed Ron in a close-call kind of way. "We will call the police at the first phone booth we see (remember phone booths?), but you girls stay in there where it's safe!" I echoed the sentiment—dish towel wrapped around my bitten wrist.

Not knowing much about rabies and timelines, we drove like crazy toward the local hospital, stopping only briefly to call the police and ask animal control to go to the apartment and flush the raccoon. I got out of the car while Ron was still pulling into a parking space and headed for the emergency room door as fast as my legs would carry me. There was a sloping lawn to navigate, and I want to tell you that running downhill can be comical, yet disastrous. My inertia carried me over top of my legs and I did a forward roll that any Olympic gymnast would be proud of. Never breaking stride, I crashed through the double door, and within minutes I was soaking in a bucket of disinfectant.

Meanwhile, back at the ranch—er, apartment—a local police officer pushed open the apartment door and coolly scanned the battlefield. Seeing no one (the girls were huddled in the bathroom) and seeing no wild animals, he creaked across the floor and nudged open the bedroom door. What he did not realize was that a miserable raccoon having a very bad day was on the other side of that barricade. With a hiss and a yelp, the coon was on the officer—taking out his fear and anger on the poor man's blue uniform. Brandishing his baton, he caught the ferocious animal with a staggering blow and quickly brought the scene under control.

Later, tests on Mr. Raccoon and Mr. Decker revealed that we were both rabies free—and I suppose we both learned a lesson. I never got to ask him about his learning experience, but as for me, it goes something like this: Wild animals are still dangerous, even if wearing a ribbon. The Bible tells us that the enemy of our soul prowls about like a roaring lion—but he disguises himself as an angel of light. We often venture too close, thinking the situation harmless—but sin always takes us further than we wanted it to go, and we often wind up with a huge conflict—out of control—in our own homes.

At this point, it's time for Dad to turn off the light and tuck in my sleepy child. As I walk downstairs I often breathe a prayer, "Lord, keep the devil far from my door—and my children. Amen."

Trumpet Lessons

"Awake, O my soul, with the music of his splendor-song!
Arise my soul and sing his praises! My worship will awaken
the dawn, greeting the daybreak with my songs of light!"
(Psalms 57:8).

I was never much of a musician, although I'm quite sure my parents wanted me to be. My sister had a knack for the piano, so it was assumed that I, too, should be good at some musical instrument. As the piano was already spoken for, I decided to take a stab at the trumpet. A worthy horn was secured at a secondhand store and lessons were established with a teenager from church who played in his high school orchestra. My eager parents even purchased a record album of a world-renowned trumpeter—in hopes that his triple tongue capabilities would rub off on me.

Over the months that followed I blurted and blatted to the best of my capabilities, rarely achieving a recognizable melody. Oftentimes I would set my music stand in the kitchen and announce that I was about to play a song, asking my mother or father to "name that tune."

My mother would respond to my playing by saying, "That sounds nice, dear, what song did you say it was?"

"I didn't say…" I would offer. "You're supposed to guess."

Yet, even after a second run through, the song would remain a mystery. "It's Happy Birthday," I would tell her. Or, "Row, Row, Row Your Boat."

"Of course," my mom would say, "very nice, dear."

"I played a sharp by mistake, instead of a flat, or else you would've gotten it," I claimed.

Then came the moment when I actually found a song that I could get through without too much difficulty. "When Morning Gilds the Skies" seemed to be in my range (it was at least recognizable in my kitchen concerto), which only could mean one thing—a solo would be upcoming in the special music spot of a Sunday night service at the church where my dad was pastor. This was serious now—I would be joining the likes of Dot Coggeshall, who was a master at the piano and organ, as well as Lorraine and Margaret, two sisters who harmonized the hymns like nobody's business. The special music slot was legendary at the church I grew up in. Now it was to be my turn.

I practiced and practiced—I could've played the song in my sleep—but when the Sunday arrived on which I was scheduled to play, I was a wreck. The trumpet felt foreign in my clammy hands and my lips only quivered when they were supposed to pucker. My legs were like jelly and I couldn't catch my breath. After about four notes, I caved in. "I can't do it," I said, looking back at my dad behind the pulpit.

"Yes you can," he encouraged. "Keep going."

There was no other option now—so I played on. I'm sure it wasn't very special to the enduring congregation, but you know, by the time I hit the second stanza, it wasn't half bad. I finished with a flourish—a high note an octave above—and sat down to appreciative applause.

"Let's all sing it together!" announced my relieved father. "Hymn number four-thirty-two, When Morning Gilds the Skies." We all stood and belted out the old hymn, with ol' Dot making the organ sound like a cathedral instrument. At that very moment, I learned the beauty of church life and the support of family—the acceptance, the love.

There have been other times since that day when my heart has pounded with anxiety. My dad is gone now, but I still can hear my Father say, "Yes you can—keep going." Onward the push, the second stanza is just ahead.

And we *will* finish with a flourish—a high note far above.

94

Surprised by Love

"However, as it is written: 'What no eye has seen, what no ear has heard, and what no human mind has conceived'—the things God has prepared for those who love Him"
(1 Corinthians 2:9 NIV).

I was completely surprised! My wife had packed our bags, made the reservations and saved some spending money—all to plan a weekend getaway for the two of us, and she did it all without me ever knowing what she was up to! What a wonderful surprise I had in store. We got in the car on a Friday afternoon to head for a meeting, and she then informed me (with a huge grin!) that the meeting she had was with me! We were headed for a nice hotel. She had arranged to have the kids all cared for, and for all the other "bases" to be covered. My only job was to relax and enjoy. I couldn't wipe the surprised smile off my face no matter how hard I tried. How wonderful it is to be so loved.

When Prudence misbehaves, she has to go into "time out"—a time of separation. If she happens to be in the car at the time, we try to remain consistent even though it involves unbuckling her car seat and having her stand outside the vehicle with one of us for a minute or two. The other day, she smacked her sister while we were in the department store parking lot. After explaining that those kinds of behaviors have consequences, we removed her from her seat to stand outside in time out. As I sat behind the wheel, mother and daughter stood in the parking lot holding hands. My heart melted as Prudence looked up, squinting in the sun, and asked, "Are you going to drive away, Mommy?" At her tender age, she is not yet able to comprehend the depths of love we have for her, the ties so strong.

I thought to myself, *I wonder if that is how our heavenly Father must feel?* He promises He will never leave nor forsake us, and yet we question His love all the time. Especially when we are going through times of discipline, our hearts wonder if He has left us. We don't understand the depths of love that would never "drive away." Instead, nails were driven into His Son's hands and feet—fastening our heart to His forever.

Someday, we will all be surprised by love, just as I was surprised by my special weekend get away, but this time it will be Jesus who has made ready the preparations. He is holding our reservation securely. We can't even imagine what He has in store for us—it is beyond any earthly hotel or mansion. But it should bring a smile to our face when we consider that God is going to such lengths to ensure that we can be together, forever. "And so shall we ever be with the Lord," the Scriptures say. And while the beauty that is yet to be revealed remains a wonderful secret, we can know for certain that we will see it someday. Trust in the Lord with all your heart. Know that Jesus is your Redeemer. How wonderful it is to be so loved.

The family of God is forever. All the arrangements are being made—right under our noses. You may be aware of a few of the details, but Someone is lovingly planning the entire getaway with you in mind. Just wait until you see the grin on His face when we catch a glimpse of heaven!

Boston Strong

"And you should imitate me, just as I imitate Christ"
(1 Corinthians 11:1 NLT).

It was April 2013. We were at our usual spot on the Boston Marathon racecourse, several miles away from the finish line. Our day was ending. We had cheered ourselves hoarse, passed out all of the orange wedges, and run out of water. We gathered our blankets and chairs and got in the truck.

Then the phone rang. It was Joe Perry, my father-in-law. "Are you all okay?" came the question. That began a deluge of social media posts and text messages as the horrible news of the Marathon Massacre unfolded.

You know, we are never very far from tragedy. We surround ourselves with comfort, building a sense of security. But just up the road, across the street, or in the next apartment, someone is struggling to stay alive, to stay hopeful, or to just stay. Sad dramas unfold all around us—just beyond our sight. Anonymous pain, private suffering, personal grief—right next door.

When terror hits, there are always two reactions. We saw them both play out on that fateful race day. Most people run away from the smoke and chaos—but some run to it. We don't have to have a bomb blast go off to realize that there are devastating situations all around us. Do we close our eyes and move quickly away to a comfort zone—or do we drop everything and rush into the blast zone of the pain and suffering? You could be someone's hero today. It doesn't take much. "Having done all—stand!" is how the apostle put it. One individual stood in the crowd at Yankee Stadium holding high a sign stating "New York loves Boston" with the Red Sox insignia boldly emblazoned under the word "Heroic." Our lives should be like that sign—telling the hurting ones that we know, we care, and we love.

The story is told of Sharkoff, the most notable prisoner the old London jail ever held. Following a life of crime, he was captured and sentenced to die on the gallows. On the eve of execution, the prison chaplain dutifully visited the prisoner in hopes that he may make some peace with God.

Taking out his Bible, the chaplain stood outside the darkened cell and began to read. "All we like sheep have gone astray—we have turned every one to his own way, and the Lord has laid on Him the iniquity of us all."

Before he could read more, the voice of Sharkoff commanded that he stop. "Do you believe that, chaplain?" the doomed man asked.

"Why, yes, sir," came the chaplain's reply.

"Read on then!" bellowed Sharkoff.

"For God so loved the world that He gave His only begotten Son, that whosoever believeth in Him could have everlasting life—"

"*Stop!*" came the prisoner's voice again. "Do you believe that, chaplain? Do you believe that word, *whosoever*?"

"Yes, sir," the chaplain answered.

"You lie! You do not believe those words *all* and *whosoever*," shot back the convict. "I grew up in this city; I lived on the streets. I have been in your churches and I never heard anyone speak of this. That any man, no matter how wretched and vile, could still be forgiven! If I believed that, I would tell everybody! But I do not believe it, and you must not believe it either. Now go away! Take your lies with you."

Early the next morning as they put the noose around his neck, they asked, "Sharkoff, do you have any last words?"

Before they sprung the trap, his final words were, "They lie. They lie. They do not believe."

Let's live like believers. Don't run from heartache that is all around us. Someone's eternity may rest on it.

At the Cross

"For this is how much God loved the world—he gave his uniquely conceived Son as a gift. So now everyone who believes in him will never perish but experience everlasting life" (John 3:16).

Every summer 'round about the beginning of August, Gunstock Mountain in New Hampshire becomes an outdoor cathedral. That's when the SoulFest music festival takes center stage for three days of Christian music. Musicians and concert-goers fill the mountainside, blankets spread like patchwork on the green grass. Vendors sell anything and everything from popcorn to T-shirts, jewelry to lattes. The event brings thousands of worshipers from all over the globe to gather as one in the open air.

At the base of the sloping mountain, just to the left of the main stage stands a wooden cross, twelve feet high. It dominates the landscape. Year after year, hundreds come to drive a nail into the rough wood of that rugged cross; each nail symbolizing a burden or a problem that hinders relationship with God. Each evening, the nails are covered with flowers, creating a beautiful image of grace. My wife and I coordinate the cross ministry. It has become an important and, indeed, beautiful place for us. There we have prayed with those struggling with addiction, the lonely, couples whose marriages were crumbling—so many stories are shared there in the shadow of the cross. None hit us harder than Kevin's true tale of sorrow.

I noticed him standing to one side of the cross, eyes on the nails but his focus a thousand miles away. Approaching him, I asked if I could pray with him. And that is how I met Kevin Kadamus. Just weeks earlier, Kevin and his son had gone hunting. It was a day like so many before as both men were seasoned outdoorsmen. They had mapped out their strategy and positions the night before, and both were confident that the plan was a good one. Taking their places at dawn they waited patiently for a flock of wild turkeys to come within their sites. Jacob, a fine athlete and a great student, loved spending time together with his dad on mornings such as these. Kevin lay in a thicket about 150 yards from his son's position. That's when he saw the movement to his right. Waiting, still, Kevin held his finger on the trigger of the shotgun. Any moment he would have a clear shot. There! Turkeys! Fire! He squeezed the trigger. What happened next was sheer horror.

Kevin heard Jacob scream, "No!" In the same second that his mind tried to comprehend the sound, he saw his boy jump up from the brush—terror on his face. He started to run, somewhere, anywhere, away from what had just happened. Within a few steps, he faltered and fell—into his father's trembling arms. "Oh, God! This didn't just happen!" cried Kevin. But it had. Jacob passed away in his father's embrace. As Kevin watched his son's life ebbing away, despair and disbelief choked his throat.

How a dad can live through that is beyond what I can comprehend. The only way to deal with the pain and loss was for us to stand together at the foot of the cross, the very place where Abba Father watched His own Son die—so many years before. Somewhere in that understanding, hope overtakes suffering and life rattles on its bittersweet course. Kevin took a nail and hammered it in deep as I stood by in silence. Just then, the skies opened and it started to rain.

Kevin and I come back each year to SoulFest. We meet at the cross. We stand together. He is my brother, after all. We share the severe love of our Father—Abba understands.

Prudence

"So when we preach that Christ was crucified, the Jews are offended and the Gentiles say it's all nonsense. But to those called by God to salvation, both Jews and Gentiles, Christ is the power of God and the wisdom of God"
(1 Corinthians 1:23-24 NLT).

Most of my conversations with my youngest daughter, Prudence, occur in my truck. It seems we are always going somewhere in that little red pickup. I call it my "Anti-matter Machine" because when I am behind the wheel all the "matters" of the day fade away, and I simply enjoy the cozy environs of the cab, following the road that stretches out ahead.

Prudence is equally at home in her familiar spot; she sits in her car seat behind the passenger front seat, and there she looks dreamily out through her window, sun splashing on her face, her head leaning against the glass. Usually it is Prudence who breaks the silence. She will often furrow her brow and toss up a real fascinating question. Today's was no different.

Pru: Is God strong?

Dad: Yes, very strong.

Pru: Can He lift up a tree?

Dad: Yes, in fact there was a time when He did carry a tree.

Pru: Really?

Dad: It was a wooden cross—as big as a tree. He was crucified on that "tree."

Pru: What's *crunesifide* mean?

Dad: Cru-ci-fied, it means they nailed Jesus to the cross. Do you know why He was on the cross?

Pru: (silence) Because people hated Him.

Dad: Who hated Him?

Pru: The soldiers.

Dad: But not us—we like Jesus, in fact we love Him.

Pru: Yeah, we love Jesus.

Dad: How much do we love Jesus?

Pru: Big much, as big as a million rocks.

As the Scripture says, "We preach Christ crucified" (1 Cor. 1:23 NIV). One day, God did carry a tree—and it made all the difference. Christ carried more than a tree though; He carried away all of our sin with it. That is the truth we love to hear come back to us through our own children. It's also the truth that the church carries to the world. It's good news for all.

Once we respond to it personally, we find that we enter into a family. However, I am afraid it's a fading concept—the importance of church—but it's there that we can practice our "one anothers" such as the New Testament instructs. There are close to twenty "one anothers" in the Scriptures. We are to love *one another*, serve *one another*, pray for *one another*, and encourage *one another*, just to name a handful. It's love for one another that causes the world to recognize that we belong to Jesus—and indeed, we also belong to one another.

Jesus started this love revolution by loving us first. We love You back Jesus—as big as a million rocks.

The Rescue

"He stooped down to lift me out of danger from the desolate pit I was in, out of the muddy mess I had fallen into. Now he's lifted me up into a firm, secure place and steadied me while I walk along his ascending path" (Psalms 40:2).

Snow's Pond in Rochester, Massachusetts is a place where I spent much of my childhood. It's a beautiful location, fine for swimming, fishing, and boating. Private homes dot the shoreline and a small island greets the eye in the middle of the scenic landscape. Every summer I fished and swam away the hours with family and friends—laying on the white sandy beach to soak up the warm sun. In midwinter, the shadows from the trees fall across the snow-covered sand while the pond becomes a hockey rink for neighborhood face-offs.

It was one hot July day back in the early '70s when I nearly lost my life at Snow's Pond. My mother insisted that her children know how to swim, dive, row a boat, and paddle a canoe. To that end, there were always swimming lessons and boating classes—as we progressed from the dog paddle to the crawl stroke. Somehow along the way we acquired an old rowboat—a wooden dory that leaked a little, but provided us with hours of fun exploring the pond's furthest points and peninsulas.

On this particular day, I was at the oars with my friend Dougie, lazing in the bow seat. We were floating mostly, chatting idly and enjoying our summer freedom. Suddenly, a moment of inspiration came to Dougie's face and he stood, announcing, "I'm Peter and there's Jesus. I'm gonna walk on water!" and over the side he went. The very next words from his mouth were more of a gasp, "Help! I can't swim!" Under the water went Dougie. Over the side I went.

Dougie's unexpected jump into the water had shoved the boat away from where he now struggled for air. His flailing body was splashing as he broke the surface. Swimming hard to where he went back under, I dove and grabbed him around the waist. Instantly, he wrapped his legs around me and held on with a panicked death grip. We both were sucking in large amounts of Snow's Pond as we went below the surface another time. I thought it was to be the last time. *We're drowning*, I thought. I watched the surface slip farther and farther away—there was nothing I could do.

Suddenly, I wasn't sinking. I was being pushed upward. A hand was underneath me, and as I broke into the fresh air—gasping—I saw that Dougie had also been rescued. Beneath the ten feet of water was Dougie's dad—walking on the bottom, arms extended above his head, pushing us both to the shore and safety. At the first glance of the trouble he ran from the beach, dove into the pond, and swam toward us with everything he had. A former US Navy man, he had practiced water rescues many times—he knew just what to do. Soon all three of us were safe on shore. Dougie's mom wrapped us in towels as we sat, shaking from our ordeal. My mom began the slow, deliberate swim to retrieve the dory.

The next day, Dougie stopped by my home with a small gift. "A thank you," he said, "for saving my life." I knew we had both been saved that prior day, and that was where thanks belonged. So, thanks again to Dougie's dad—all these years later, I still remember what you did that day.

I don't know what you are drowning in, what holds you in a death grip—be it an addiction or an unhealthy relationship. But I know there is an Unseen Hand beneath you—pushing up, up, to break free. Now, breathe.

Boomer

"If you tenderly care for this little child on my behalf, you are tenderly caring for me. And if you care for me, you are honoring my Father who sent me. For the one who is least important in your eyes is actually the most important one of all" (Luke 9:48).

Perception is reality, I often say—and perspective is a personal thing. We travel through our lives seeing things the way we see them. We rarely consider the fact that everyone sees things differently. We just don't think the same thoughts. My wife and I play a little game at random moments where we ask each other the question, "What song is playing in your head right now?" Over the years, we have posed the question hundreds of times—never have we had the same answer. The melody rattling around in my brain is not the one she has in hers—ever. Individuals see (and hear) things differently.

When my son Brett was young, he had to go to a major hospital in Boston for tests. Brett was a rambunctious boy. We nicknamed him "Boomer" because he was always going "*boom!*" and he had the bruises to prove it. His curly blonde hair framed a face full of yellowing bruises and fresh scratches—and every day it was part of life's adventure to see what mischief Brett would get into.

On our first trip into Boston for Brett's initial visit to the hospital we got up early and headed up the expressway toward the city. As we rounded a big curve, the city of Boston came into full view—skyscrapers stretching out before us—a panorama to behold. "Wooooah!" breathed little Boomer. "Knock 'em all down, Daddy!"

His child's eye perspective from the rear of our family van made it seem as though the mammoth buildings were no bigger than his building blocks. I had often seen Brett crash his toy cars into any number of things in our home—this was just more of the same to him. In Brett's world, the giant buildings of Boston would crumble at the push of my bumper. I suppose when you have a child's perspective, anything is possible. Dad can do anything.

When Brett's sister Mercedes was in kindergarten, it was a difficult time for me as Dad. I was singlehandedly raising my five children. Life was a complex mix of babysitters, ministry, school lunches, and dirty dishes. As I look back, I can picture myself, dog tired, leaning against the dryer waiting for it to end its cycle so I could have the kids in clean clothes for school the next morning. Often, when the buzzer sounded it would startle me awake.

Mercedes was my youngest child then, and her kindergarten class was delightful. I always picked her up after school, and I enjoyed blending in with other moms and dads, discussing any number of parental topics. One day, I stood in line to collect her after the school day was over and saw that her teacher was walking her out, apparently to tell me something. I hoped she hadn't misbehaved—it seemed unlikely, but nevertheless, I adopted my most pastoral demeanor and waited.

"We learned all about Dr. Martin Luther King today," said her teacher, putting Mercedes' hand in mine. "We learned that he was a great leader and a man of peace. I also told the class that Dr. King was a minister—just like…" She paused and went on with the leading question, "Mercedes, what does your daddy do?"

The words floated in the air as my daughter pondered. Then Mercedes announced, "Laundry!" My five year old figured I did laundry for a living. I guess dads can do anything in a child's perception of things. I reckon even MLK had his days waiting for that dryer to signal the end of the cycle—and I am doubly sure that was not the end of the dirty clothes. The basket of the waiting-to-be-washed laundry always looms like a tower in the corner—mounds of clothes. Knock 'em all down, Daddy.

Snipe Hunt

"So keep your thoughts continually fixed on all that is authentic and real, honorable and admirable, beautiful and respectful, pure and holy, merciful and kind. And fasten your thoughts on every glorious work of God, praising him always" (Philippians 4:8).

I belonged to the "Boy's Club" at our church during my growing up years. There were always fifteen to twenty young men in the "pack," and every Tuesday evening we would gather for a couple of hours' worth of Bible lessons and games like "Capture the Flag" or "Steal the Bacon."

Occasionally, we would venture outside and take some unsuspecting newbie on a "snipe hunt"—a search for a mythical bird so rarely sighted and yet rumored to be nesting in the area. As we stomped through the weeds and woods we kept a sharp eye out for the elusive snipe—of course we were all clued in to the ruse (there was no snipe), and gradually one by one we would secretly drop from the pack and return to the church building. Meanwhile, our unsuspecting hunter of rare birds looked in earnest, making snipe-like noises and shining the flashlight all around the grounds. Soon, the victim of our bird-prank was searching on his own, so engrossed in the hunt that he had no clue that the rest of the crew were sitting in the church basement, sipping soda pop and munching brownies. After a while (sometimes a long while!), the awareness would dawn on the youth that he was alone. Unsettled and unsure what to make of his plight—he would scamper back to the church where the boys sat waiting. "Find any snipe?" someone would ask—and the snickering would begin.

As the confused lad began to put two and two together, the snickers would become guffaws as the jokesters rolled on the floor in hysterics. "There is no such thing as a snipe," our leader would inform the embarrassed young man. "You spent the last hour and a half in a complete waste of time! Snipe are imaginary, they aren't real."

I think some of us chase "snipe" for much of our lives. We imagine that we are going to purchase that golden lottery ticket. We dream of Mr. or Mrs. Right logging on to the singles network at just the right moment. We imagine the perfect job or the house with the white picket fence.

Not only do we imagine happy endings, but much of our personal frustration is imagined as well. We could avoid many negative emotions that battle within us if we steered clear of imagined situations. Most of us know what this is like. We are at odds with someone, let's say a co-worker, and we find ourselves avoiding them. In our imagination however, we construct entire conversations with that person. We imagine what we would say to them and then provide their retort with an "I know what they would say." We then shoot back with a sassy answer, thinking, "I'd like to tell them this!" We work our emotions into a lather, getting more and more angry—and none of it has actually happened! It's all imaginary. Snipe! When we awaken at 3 a.m. with a jolt of conscience, we often play out the next day with encounters and arguments that have yet to occur—and, in reality, may never happen. More snipe!

So, I say—stick to reality. Deal with the actual. The more time you spend with the truth, the less likely you will find yourself wasting time searching for something in the dark.

Under the Boardwalk

"Take away the filthy garments from him. And unto him he said, Behold, I have caused thine iniquity to pass from thee"
(Zechariah 3:4 KJV).

There once was a businessman who worked in a port city. His office overlooked the beach and boardwalk, where crowds of people shopped and sunned, enjoying the waterfront activities. The man was a diligent and successful worker. and his staff admired him. The businessman had a routine. Every day, the family nanny brought his four-year-old son to have lunch with him. These were precious times for the man—his lunch hour with his son. "No calls, please," he would say over his shoulder to his secretary. And out the door they would go, arm in arm. They often climbed down a back staircase, emerging from a wooden gate and out onto the beach. They could stroll along under the shade of the boardwalk and feel the cool mist off the ocean or walk the sunny beach and feel the hot sand on their toes. Gone for an hour each midday, his staff knew how important this lunch hour ritual was to both man and boy.

There was one place under the wooden walkway that the man and boy would always avoid—a bench that served as the usual station of a certain homeless man. He wore tattered clothing. He was caked in sweat and dirt. His ever-present brown bag suggested he was rarely sober. "Don't look, son." the businessman would say as they gave the poor stranger a wide berth.

However, one day things were just a little different. The businessman was expecting an important client to call; the deal they would discuss was worth millions of dollars. "If he calls," he nodded at his receptionist, "forward the call to my cell phone. I need to connect with that gentleman today!" With that, he and his little boy went out the door and down to the beach. They started walking as was their usual routine. They ordered a couple of hot dogs and a soda pop and enjoyed the casual lunch. It was almost time to go back to the office when the man's cell phone signaled a call was coming through. Sure enough, it was the million-dollar call.

For a few minutes his attention was entirely on the phone call. Absorbed in the details, he secured an agreement and ended the call. But now where was his son? He scanned the crowd of people and saw no sign of his boy. Hurriedly, he strode through the mass of people, his eyes scanning everywhere. Fear was rising in his throat. He noticed a commotion down by the ocean edge—people waving their arms, pointing to something caught in the waves. Could it be? A sense of horror seized him. Before his feet could move, a lone figure dashed across the sand and dove into the water. As he ran closer he could clearly see the rescue that was taking place. He got to the water's edge just as a small boy—his boy—was being stretched out on the sand. He stood with the onlookers as the man who pulled the child from the sea breathed life back into his lungs.

Gathering his son into his arms, he turned to thank the rescuer. Amazingly, he found himself looking in to the face of the homeless man from under the boardwalk. The man he had taught his son to fear had just given him back his life.

From that day forward the man and his son continued their lunchtime tradition, but no longer did they walk past the homeless man with his dirty clothes and his brown bag. Now they would stop and visit, sharing a hot dog or a sandwich. When asked why he chose to spend time with someone like that, he would always explain, "When I look at that man, I do not see his filth and grime. When I look at that man, I see my son."

In the Old Testament, the ancient prophet Zechariah saw a vision of Joshua, the high priest, standing before the Lord. Satan stands close by, accusing Joshua of being stained and dirty. The Lord emphatically rebukes the enemy, stating that he has been made clean.

God doesn't see your stain of sin, nor your lost condition. No, when He looks at you, He sees His Son.

The Burden

"Love empowers us to fulfill the law of the Anointed One as we carry each other's troubles" (Galatians 6:2).

We aren't always patient with one another; and yet, it is one of the key attributes of our faith—to be patient. We are destined to be people who can carry a load and not collapse under its weight. What really encourages patience is for us to remember this truth—the one you are impatient with may be suffering an unimaginable hardship.

Such was the case many years ago in one of our nation's major cities. The story unfolds along the corridors of a hospital in that city. Two couples were there, each with a desperately ill child. Day after day they kept vigil over their bedridden little loved ones. At night, they paced the floor of the housing facility where families were allowed to stay when a child underwent an extended time period in the hospital. As the days turned into weeks, they formed a fast friendship such as is often the case when people go through trials together. They ate every meal together, always offering encouragement or solace depending on the prognosis report of that day.

As time passed, it became obvious that one child was improving while the other was slipping further and further toward death. The families both knew that it was only a matter of time. One child would be going home. The other would soon pass away. That fateful day came on a wintry November weekend. The doctor had called in the middle of the night to let the parents know their little son was indeed dead. Having spent all of their resources, they found that they could not afford to fly their child's body back to their home in the Midwest for burial. Instead, they wrapped him in a blanket, and despite unimaginable grief had to place the body of their son in the trunk of their car to make the long drive home.

Blinded by tears, they bade goodbye to the couple they had grown to love, holding their little girl who was discharged that same day. As they pulled out of the driveway onto the busy city thoroughfare an impatient driver leaned on his horn and screamed obscenities out the window. "How awful," exclaimed the mother standing in the driveway, still crying and waving goodbye. "If that driver only knew what they carried in their trunk."

Most people consider the Old Testament when they think of laws in the Bible. But Jesus had one too—we are to look out for one another and bear each other's burdens. When we focus on ourselves, patience tends to run thin with others. Yet if we truly see others and the burdens they carry (the secret ones they don't talk about), our hearts rise with the compassion of Jesus. I often put it this way: we all have a need meter, but what we need to be are "need-meeters." If your own need-meter is maxed out you'll only see that which you think can help you. The trick is to get busy helping others and meeting their needs; you'll find that patience follows naturally. And so, be patient with everyone you meet. You just never know what sort of burden they are carrying.

The Question

*"Lord, even when your path takes me through the valley
of deepest darkness, fear will never conquer me, for you
already have! You remain close to me and lead me through
it all the way. Your authority is my strength and my peace"*
(Psalms 23:4).

There once was a preacher who in the 1950s became known to many as a Bible Answer Man. His knowledge of Scripture was so vast that he would often take on the hardest questions of scholarly skeptics and within minutes provide an answer that would amaze the listener. He could tackle any question. Any question at all.

That is until his beloved wife died suddenly, leaving him with three small children to raise alone. Now the man with all of the answers suddenly had nothing but questions. How could God let this happen? How was he going to parent his children as a single dad? But the toughest question of all came on the way to the cemetery as he and the children rode in the limousine. Holding tightly to his little girl's hand he bent low to hear her whisper, "Daddy, did it hurt Mommy when she died?" His heart broke. Breathless, speechless, he turned his face to the window to hide the torrent of tears.

Just at that moment, a large truck went by heading in the opposite direction. Passing by the funeral procession, it momentarily cast a shadow over the vehicles as it blocked the evening sunlight. The bereaved preacher had his answer.

Turning to his daughter he asked, "Did you see that truck pass by?"

"Yes, Daddy," she answered.

"Did it hurt us as it drove past?" he countered.

"No," said the little girl.

"Right you are," he went on. "The truck passed by us, but only the shadow touched us. And so it is with death. Jesus went before us and suffered the full impact of death. Now, we only walk through its shadow."

Believers die differently. We do not hold tightly to the things of this earth—for like death itself, they are just passing shadows. The Light is shining, over there.

Closed on Sunday

*"For I delivered to you as of first importance what I also
received: that Christ died for our sins in accordance with the
Scriptures"* (1 Corinthians 15:3 ESV).

Some stories need to be told—this is one of them. It happened many years ago, and it goes something like this.

There was a certain radio evangelist whose gospel program was listened to all over the nation. Featuring music and the spoken word, the broadcast became popular. Soon speaking engagements were being requested, and thus, on many weekends, he would travel to churches around the country. He often brought a musician along to recreate the dynamics of the program right there in the church. He was so successful that he was soon traveling most weekends. To help deal with the demand, he went into a recording studio and produced a record album featuring his preaching on one side of the disc, and on the other side a vocalist recorded some of the favorite melodies from the radio show. To places he had not gone the record was the "next best thing." In places where he did travel, the album served as a keepsake for many who purchased them.

One weekend, he was ministering at a church in the conservative Southwest. All was going well until the radio host asked for a table to be placed in the rear of the auditorium so that he could set up a display and sell the sought-after record albums. The host pastor flatly denied his request. When asked why, he stated, "We won't sell items on Sunday." Respectful of the pastor's position, the visiting radio preacher offered, "Why not give them to whoever would like one and simply ask them to mail a check to us sometime this coming week?" It seemed like a good proposal, so the agreement was made. Within a very short time the albums were gone and the display empty of merchandise.

Upon returning home he instructed his secretary to keep an eye on the mailbox, expectant of a large number of checks from the area where he had just ministered. Based on the number of records they had distributed it was bound to be a productive week financially. But at week's end came the report—nothing. The second week, nothing, and the third was the same. A month went by and still not a single check was received. In fact, no checks ever arrived.

"If they ever invite me back, be sure and tell them yes," he instructed his staff. "When they ask for a sermon title, tell them I will be preaching on the topic: Which is worse—selling things on Sunday or stealing them?"

That story causes me to wince a bit. We so want to do things right—but we all fall short. Back in the days of my childhood, I recall most businesses were closed on Sunday, but in our materialistic society of today it has become just another shopping day. However, I am not here to bring back Sunday store closings. I am here to defend the gospel. And that is always free—every day of the week.

A Gift Gone Wrong

"To the lonely, he gives a family. To the prisoner, he leads into prosperity until they each sing for joy" (Psalms 68:6a).

I had a peaceful and pleasant upbringing. I think times were simpler then, back in the 1960s. Or maybe it just seems so. Today, fifty years later, social media and around-the-clock news bring the world to our doorstep in unrelenting waves of information. Back then the Internet was a dream, and twenty-four hour news networks were an impossibility. Perhaps *sheltered* comes forth as a better word than *simpler*. I had a sheltered childhood. News from beyond came slowly and was served to us tastefully. Picture Walter Cronkite at the news desk reading copy versus today's news reporter on the battlefront, directly in harm's way. The savagery of hate and violence once came to our television and radio in measured doses from around the globe. Now it pours in unchecked over social media sites.

The outside world back then seemed safer. But there is an inside world to consider as well—the goings-on inside one's home. I'm sure that I was sheltered there as well. My father was a minister. My mom was an artist. Dad spent hours in the preparation of sermons and Mom spent hours in front of the canvas. They got along well; it was a peaceful home. But I recall one day that was different.

It was my mother's birthday and I wanted to purchase a gift for her. I had saved enough allowance money to get something on my own, and so my dad agreed to drive me to a nearby department store in New Bedford to hunt for the perfect present. Somehow an electric coffee pot caught my eye—on sale! Dad checked, and sure enough I had the necessary funds.

The purchase made, I held the treasured pot in my lap all the way home—imagining my mom's delight when she saw this new, wonderful gift. It didn't play out that way.

Apparently my mom had quite a collection of coffee pots. Upon opening my latest addition, she burst into tears. I was stymied as I watched her go to the cupboards and the spare room closet, pulling out coffee makers of all sorts and kinds—while my dad sat dumbfounded, no doubt regretting that he had not steered me clear of kitchen appliances back at the department store. I was devastated. I ran to my room and cried—the chooser of the worst present ever.

Looking back, I can see that there were other pressures that weighed on my parents that night. But at seven years of age, the blame for the outburst settled in my own heart. It was my fault. I bought the coffee pot that made my mother cry and made my parents argue. Case closed. Guilty.

How fortunate I am that this one episode stands alone in my memories of childhood. Call it a bad night, an off day. But some of you reading this had family chaos and confusion playing out every night and every day. Many times you found yourself crying alone in your room while raised voices carried through the walls, pounding in like bad news from abroad. And here's a thought: you probably blamed yourself for the commotion. Somehow, in the turmoil, an evil finger pointed at your tender heart and said, "You are to blame." But that's a lie. The evil one does not tell the truth. He intends harm. He wreaks havoc. He knocks apart families.

Always remember that just down the street or around the corner there is a family waiting to welcome you. The book of Psalms states that God puts the lonely in families. Perhaps it is time to let Him put you into yours. It just may be the shelter you need. We call it church.

Phone Booth

"You perceive every movement of my heart and soul, and understand my every thought before it even enters my mind. You are so intimately aware of me, Lord. You read my heart like an open book and you know all the words I'm about to speak before I even start a sentence! You know every step I will take before my journey even begins!" (Psalms 139:2-4).

As far as I can determine, this story really happened. Many years ago, there was a growing church in the northwest corner of our country. Each week, visitors flocked to listen to the gifted pastor. We will call him Pastor Ken. He was a powerful speaker and was known for always giving an altar call at the close of each Sunday sermon. Many responded to his invitations, and thus there was growing spiritual excitement in the region.

Pastor Ken would be out in the streets during the week, evangelizing and making friends with the city dwellers who populated the area. On one such afternoon, a lonely young woman listened as Pastor Ken shared the gospel in a tiny coffee shop.

No one present that afternoon could see the inner anguish of this woman, but as she strained to catch every word; she knew she needed the hope the preacher spoke of. Several times she had considered suicide, and even now she was dangerously close to trying to bring an end to her life. That night, back in her apartment, she searched the phone book for the church listing where she could locate Pastor Ken and his words of hope. Finding the number, she placed a call and asked what time the

Sunday morning service started. "It's my last chance," she reasoned, and she made plans to attend the following Sunday.

Sunday came, and she found herself at the door to the church. She was warmly greeted, ushered to a seat, and handed a brochure. Before long the service began. She was soon lost in the beauty of the music. She listened to each word that Pastor Ken spoke and at the end of the sermon her heart pounded in her chest as he gave the invitation to come to the altar to receive Jesus. "Getting saved" sounded like the rescue her soul needed, but fear kept her in her seat. "I'll come back next week and go forward then," she decided.

The week dragged by. Never had seven days seemed so long. But Sunday came at last, and the young woman finally found herself back at the church, ready and willing to give her heart to Jesus at the close of the pastor's message.

Little did she know that Pastor Ken had received a telephone call in the early hours of that Sunday morning, stating that his father-in-law was hospitalized and close to death. He had only days, if not hours, to live. "Pack a bag, Honey!" he told his wife. "We'll leave right after church is over."

Their intention was to drive straight through the night and into the morning, arriving at the hospital around noon on Monday. With a nearly twenty-four hour drive ahead of him, he was rather un-focused on the morning service—and in a desire to be on the road as soon as possible, he shortened his sermon and did not offer his standard altar call invitation. Meanwhile, the young woman sat perplexed. Crestfallen, she exited the church building wondering what she should do now. "He didn't ask us to come forward!" she lamented." Now, what can I do?" Thoughts of suicide came rushing in.

Sadly, she returned to her apartment. At that same hour, Ken checked the clock in the family van. "We should be in Ohio by 1 p.m. tomorrow," he told his wife, sitting beside him. "We're making good time."

Monday morning dawned. In the dim light of her city apartment, the suicidal young lady had an idea. "I will call and make an appointment to see Pastor Ken," she said, dialing the church number on her telephone. The receptionist who answered had not yet seen the hastily written note from Pastor Ken, explaining he would be gone for several days on a family emergency.

"He's not in the office," explained the receptionist, "but you can probably catch him at home. Here's the number." Ready to try anything, she frantically dialed Pastor Ken's home number.

Meanwhile, halfway across the country, Ken and his wife stopped at a convenience store to gas up and to grab some snacks. "You go ahead inside," Ken said. "I'm going to stretch my legs." Beyond the spacious parking lot were some railroad tracks with a pathway alongside. The tired minister began walking, happy to be out of the car for a few minutes. As he strolled past a telephone booth, he was startled to hear it ringing. Unsure of what to do, he dutifully lifted the receiver off of the hook. "Hello?" he said, his curiosity piqued.

"Pastor Ken?" said a frail voice on the other end of the line. Confused, he stammered out a yes and soon discovered that the woman on the other end of the line was in deep need. He spoke words of hope to her, prayed with her, and promised to meet with her in a couple of days.

"How did you get this number?" he asked her.

"Your secretary at the church gave it to me," she answered. "I'm sorry to call you at home."

"Home?" he chuckled. "Not only am I not at home—I'm at a phone booth somewhere in Wyoming. That's how much God cares for you." Astonished, he explained to the woman why he was alongside the Interstate, many miles from home. After thanking God for His love and care, Ken went back to his van and sat next to his wife.

"Y'know?" he mused, "God knows *exactly* where I am."

I have a good friend who always says, "Be open to God wherever you may be." God loves to rescue people—and if you have already been rescued, you can be certain He will involve you in the plan to save another. He knows just where to find you.

One Christmas

"Every gift God freely gives us is good and perfect, streaming down from the Father of Lights, who shines from the heavens with no hidden shadow or darkness and is never subject to change" (James 1:17).

We get pretty engrossed in our daily circumstances. In fact, we often let them dictate our moods and our behavior. That's not how it supposed to be. Day-to-day situations come and go—they change like the wind—but that which holds us together needs to be strong and consistent. In other words, we cannot draw our daily strength from our environment. Our strength must come from a different source. Life is bound to jostle us a bit. There are flat tires, flu bugs, unexpected expenses, supper to cook, and dishes to be done. Those are but minor things that derail us. What about the bigger problems? A wayward teenager, cancer, automobile accidents—those are tough to handle. Expand it even further—there are natural disasters, famines, and wars. We dare not rely on this world for sustaining power with which to endure.

I often ask people to picture life this way. You are given a large straw and placed before two deep wells. One well is filled with clear, cold, fresh water. The other is foul and rancid, polluted in every way. You are given the choice which well you will draw sustenance from. The stagnant, polluted well is what the world has to offer. The fresh, crisp, and clean water comes from the throne of God. Which one will you put your straw in? From where will you gain your strength today?

The spiritual well of fresh water offers life-giving strength that will equip us to handle any problem that comes against us. Surely we will be tested. Remember, life and its problems are only a temporary matter. The strength God provides comes from heaven above. It is born in eternity. It is manufactured on high. It is built to last.

I recall one Christmastime of many years ago. For weeks leading up to the holiday, I had been lobbying hard for an electric race car set. It was about all I could think of. I pleaded with my parents. I brought it up at every family meal. My folks would patiently listen and then try to move me on to other things. "How is school going?" or "Did you finish your homework?" they would ask. But I was transfixed with the dream of an oval track and speedy racing cars zooming around the turns, my hand on the accelerator.

Christmas morning finally came and I was up early. I watched the big clock in our front room until it was nearly seven. "Close enough," I reasoned, and I began the process of waking the house. Breakfast lasted for hours it seemed. As soon as the dishes were cleared, I made a beeline for the Christmas tree. A quick study of the gift-wrapped packages under the tree was not encouraging. I saw no big boxes, such as might contain a race car set. It got worse from there. Every gift seemed to have my sister's name on it. I wistfully opened a new pair of slippers, but she was pulling down big stuff—dolls and doll houses (complete with accessories!) and a kid sized oven that could really cook. There were simply no big-ticket items for me to open. Not a one. I managed to hold in the tears until my dad said, "I guess that's all." That broke the dam and torrents poured from my eyes.

Taking me by the hand, my dad said something about one more gift that he forgot to wrap. Dutifully I followed him to the guest room. He opened the door with a smile and there before me was an oval track that took up most of the floor. Two shiny race cars were perched at the starting line just waiting for me to press the trigger on the accelerator. It was magnificent! My morning of disappointment melted and disappeared in that instant.

The unseen is real—as real as that race car set in the guest room. But our present circumstances distract us and keep us from trusting our heavenly Father. My dad would never have loaded up one child with gifts while neglecting another child in the process. God won't forget either. He adores you. We too often allow our disappointments to control us as we wade through our sea of circumstances. The Father has gone to great lengths to prepare an incredible gift for you. He has set eternity in our hearts. That truth should give us strength to endure. When the situation at hand seems dire, anchor deep in the eternal nature of God. He holds the long view. What He has waiting is actual and it is real. Dry those tears and take your Father's hand. See what He has set up—just out of sight—just for you.

Microphone Check

"So this is my command: Love each other deeply, as much as I have loved you" (John 15:12).

J ohn 13:35 states, "By this everyone will know that you are my disciples, if you love one another" (NIV). God has always had an agenda for the world, and it is simple. He loves it. Heart wrenching, outpouring, magnanimous love—love to die for. God also has an agenda for the church. It also is simple to consider. It is to love like He does, "A new command I give you: Love one another. As I have loved you, so you must love one another" (John 13:34 NIV). The love God has for the world is to be practiced within the church so that the world can see True Love and be drawn into a relationship with the very Source of Love. God is love.

People in churches often lament that there is little love shown in the family. Within the pews of Christendom there is bickering and arguing. Church splits are commonplace occurrences. Here is a teaching to consider. The reason we know (and show) little love within the church is that we do not have the Lord's heart for the world outside. Love for the outsider just isn't strong enough a purpose for us to constrain our own behavior. If the world mattered more to us, we would love each other more. That word in John 13:35 that reads *everyone* means just that—the whole world. We would care more about the "one another" in the second half of that verse if we cared more about the "everyone" in the first half. In the book of Revelation, the church at Ephesus was warned that they had lost their first love. I believe that was an indictment that spoke of their waning love for the world. Like Sodom in the Old Testament, they closed their ears to the cries of the poor and looked after their own needs first. Self always comes second in the kingdom when things are running right.

One day many years ago, some ladies visited a pastor friend of mine. Along with being a pastor, he hosted a radio program right from his home. His studio was set up in the breezeway, and from his desk there he could broadcast to thousands of listeners. Well, these ladies had come for a visit to discuss some people in the church. While they waited in the breezeway for the pastor, they started the "discussion" on their own. The pastor, who was getting the tea ready in the kitchen, could hear them clearly as they ransacked individual after individual. Finally, hearing enough, he entered the room and walked over to his radio gear, "Before we get started, let me turn off the microphone," he said. "You just never know who may be listening on the other end." That cut the visit short.

We are to live and love as though the microphone is on. The world is tuning in, and the Lord is pretty clear on what our message is supposed to be. Love—enough said.

Route 9

The traffic was heavy on that Friday evening in Framingham, Massachusetts. Route 9 was a sea of headlights as I stood on the roadside—waiting to cross. It was an "end of April" kind of day, I was twenty-four years old, and spring fever had grabbed hold of my friends and me. Looking for some weekend fun, we had decided on a local restaurant as our starting place for the night. When we arrived, the wait for seating was about ninety minutes. "Let's check out the place across the street," said one of my friends. "It doesn't usually get too crowded."

We stood looking for a break in the traffic, cars whizzing past. There was a blinking yellow light fifty yards to my left, so I trotted up to see if there was a crosswalk. Meanwhile, my friends dashed across the highway, leaving me on the roadside alone. Incredibly, two lanes of travelers then slowed to a stop to let me cross. Waving my thanks, I stepped into the street and jogged toward the median. I did not realize there was a third lane, and I reached the open pavement about the same time as a sedan going forty miles per hour.

The impact was brutal. I spun onto the hood and then the roof—smashing the windshield with my head. (As I typed these words, with first-grader Prudence reading over my shoulder, she began to stroke my forehead. "I'm so sad for you," she said sweetly. "Why, Honey?" I asked. "Because you bumped your head." For a moment I thought it was well

131

worth the pain of years ago just to have this moment now with my little girl.)

I thought I was being run over. I knew I was moving fast and hitting pavement with every twist and turn. What I learned later was that I had been catapulted off the front of the screeching car as the driver applied the brakes, too late. My shoes were found two hundred feet from the point of impact. When I finally rolled to a stop I tried to stand, but a severely broken leg buckled under me.

All was still for a moment. And then she was there, her gentle voice broke the silence. "Loren, you've been hit by a car, but I am here to take care of you until help arrives." As she spoke, the woman dressed in white gathered me up and cradled my bleeding head in her lap. The two of us sat alone in the middle of the highway. I don't recall anything else she said that night, but her words brought comfort and peace. As the ambulance pulled up, she vanished into the crowd of onlookers. After she disappeared, it struck me—"How did she know my name?" I am certain that when I reach heaven I will recognize the voice of my guardian angel—and that same peace I knew the night I was stricken on a dark road will reign again, forever.

Conclusion

Now, you have reached the end of this book of modern parables. My prayer is that the love that lives in heaven is yours, that you discover that your heavenly Father is very fond of you, and that all of life points toward Him.

I trust that you will find your own place of worship to love as I love mine. It is in church where stories like these come to life. The church bears the good news to this world—that we are truly loved. As we embrace and share that love, this old globe—and indeed the universe beyond—will know that we are followers of the Shepherd. We know no other way. And so I leave you for now with these words, words to a hymn I wrote for my beloved family at LifeHouse and for you holding this book. I love you, Church.

> Upon the narrow road we trod
> Not the broad way of disbelief.
> We seek to follow after God
> And walk the way that leads to life.
>
> A tender Shepherd guides our way
> His bruised and bleeding hands we know.
> He speaks our name, we know His voice
> And follow where He bids us go.
>
> Few there be who find this road
> For heavy is the burdensome weight
> That the dear Savior does require.
> A cross is carried to heaven's gate.

Fear not the weight—turn not away
For grace has surely made it plain.
Yes, once the Savior passed this way
And all alone He bore our pain.

Oh, pilgrim would you travel too
As on this upward path we walk?
We've found such peace, we know such joy
The tender Shepherd and His flock.

About the Author

Loren Paul Decker has spent a lifetime in the ministry. He grew up as a preacher's kid and eventually found his way into Christian broadcasting. He produced and co-hosted a nationally syndicated radio program with Dr. John DeBrine for two decades before taking a full-time pastorate in Middleboro, Massachusetts. Today he is the senior pastor at LifeHouse Church in Middleboro. Loren is happily married to his wife, Amanda. Eight children make his home a place of chaotic joy— Ash, Brett, Evangeline, Lane, Mercedes, Prudence, True, and Rory.

For more information contact:
Loren Paul Decker
P.O. Box 412
Freetown, MA 02717

Website: www.iloveyouchurch.com

CPSIA information can be obtained at www.ICGtesting.com
Printed in the USA
BVOW06s0223160716

455528BV00004B/14/P